Circles of Stone

Circles of Stone

The Prehistoric Rings of Britain & Ireland

Max Milligan

Text by Aubrey Burl

THE HARVILL PRESS
LONDON

This work is affectionately dedicated to my parents: my mother Mhairi and my late father Patrick who must see it from the other side of the stones

First published in 1999 in Great Britain by
The Harvill Press
2 Aztec Row
Berners Road
London N1 0PW

www.harvill.com

First impression

Photographs copyright © Max Milligan, 1999
Text copyright © Aubrey Burl, 1999

All the site maps are due north

The authors have asserted their moral rights

A CIP catalogue record for this book
is available from the British Library

ISBN 1 86046 661 3

Designed by Isambard Thomas

Originated, printed and bound in Italy,
by EBS Verona

Part I
Early Stone Circles
*c.*3200–2500 BC

Late Neolithic to Early Bronze Age

Part II
Middle Period Stone Circles
*c.*2500–2000 BC

Early Bronze Age

Part III
Late Stone Circles
*c.*2000–1200 BC

Early to Middle Bronze Age

Introduction

Circles of stone have a long history. Ninety generations of now-forgotten people saw their construction, celebrated, entreated and buried valuable articles in them, looked to the magic of the sun and moon, and ultimately allowed them to be abandoned in the drizzle and darkness of worsening weather. This book will attempt to show their birth, record their grandeur and reveal their last moments. It is both a gallery and a history.

Between about 3500 BC and 1200 BC there were three important phases. The earliest stone circles were erected in the Late Neolithic period when metal was unknown in Britain and Ireland. They were built on moors and hillsides around the coasts of the Irish Sea and alongside the seaways between eastern Ireland and Orkney. Rings such as Swinside in the Lake District, the Ring of Brodgar in Orkney or the boulder-circles in the Carrowmore cemetery of Co. Sligo were few but large and impressive. They were over 100 feet across, their stones shoulder to shoulder like a wall surrounding an open space with a single entrance. Such a setting, although now partly collapsed, can be seen on the SE circumference of the Rollright Stones in Oxfordshire. Beyond these entrances there was sometimes a standing stone, perhaps an ancient trackway marker, centuries older than its neighbouring circle.

The rings were not just meeting places as temples for the celebration of festivals. Some were also staging posts for the trading of axes made from the specially hard stone of "factories" in the Lake District, Land's End, north Wales and northern Ireland. In the ever-expanding network of trade routes from England, Scotland, Ireland and Wales, axes from the Langdale Mountains of the Lake District were passed from depôt to depôt, down from the mountains to Castlerigg stone circle, from there eastwards to Long Meg and Her Daughters on the way to the earthwork henges of Yorkshire. Other precious axes were taken southwards to Arbor Low in the Peak District, on to the Rollright Stones in Oxfordshire and ultimately to Avebury in north Wessex, over two hundred miles of portage, following ridgeway routes along which great stone circles were comfortably positioned a few days' travel from each other.

Such vast enclosures were for large gatherings at special times of the year, these days known through alignments signposted in the circle by a taller stone, an outlying pillar or a pillar decorated with carvings. In later decades the long axis of megalithic ellipses provided an even more accurate sightline.

The study of archaeoastronomy as it is known underwent a long period of scepticism before being accepted by archaeologists. In 1723 William Stukeley observed that the avenue at Stonehenge was almost in line with the midsummer sunrise, but he had no immediate successors in the search for sightlines. Only at the commencement of the twentieth century did serious research begin.

In 1906 Sir Norman Lockyer, Director of the Solar Physics Laboratory, wrote "In continuation of my work on the astronomical uses of the Egyptian Temples I have from time to time . . . given attention to some of the stone circles and other stone monuments erected, as I believed, for similar uses in this country." His book of that year stimulated interest. Unfortunately the interest came from enthusiasts whose slapdash investigations and rash claims left archaeologists unconvinced. It was not until 1967, with the publication of Alexander Thom's *Megalithic Sites in Britain*, filled with diagrams, formulae and statistics, that properly conducted surveys began.

It is one of the ironies of archaeoastronomy that thirty years after Thom's seminal book, most of his theories, though not discredited, have been severely modified. It cannot be questioned, however, that his work led to the establishment of rigorous criteria for astronomical studies and it can now confidently be stated that great rings such as Castlerigg and Long Meg and Her Daughters had sightlines to the sun built into them whereas Scottish recumbent circles like Balquhain were designed to incorporate alignments to the southern moon. The concern with solar and lunar associations continued from the first phase of stone circles, in varying forms and with declining accuracy, throughout the history of the rings.

In the second phase, around 2500 BC, at the beginning of the Early Bronze Age, with the development in metal-working, some of the most perfect of all circles were constructed. There were giants like Stanton Drew in Somerset over 300 feet across although most were much smaller ranging from 60 feet to 100 feet in size.

What imperfect evidence exists suggests that particularly in England the majority of circles were for relatively small numbers of people, a few families gathering together from the surrounding countryside. North-eastern Scotland was different. There the rings known as recumbent stone circles crowd together in "territories" of four to six square miles, capable of supporting no more than a single family, limited to a community of about twenty men, women and children.

Architecture varied from region to region. There were circles, there were ovals. Occupants of different regions had preferred numbers for the stones in a ring – twelve in the Lake District, thirteen in the Outer Hebrides, four, six and eight in central Scotland and, as far south as Land's End, anything from nineteen to twenty-two.

Designs differed. Some circles were single, some were paired, some trebled and others in larger groups like Machrie Moor and Beaghmore. There were concentric circles, circles with long avenues leading to them, some had earthen banks in which the stones were set; some were delicately graded with the stones rising gently in height towards the SW and the setting moon. Others had shallow round depressions ground into the stones. These "cupmarks" were believed to be symbols of the sun or moon. Such architectural diversity is so noticeable and intriguing that there are surprises and delights wherever there are megalithic rings.

In the NE of Scotland the group of fascinating rings mentioned above had a huge, long and low block laid flat on the ground between the two tallest pillars of the ring. These recumbent stone circles, Loanhead of Daviot being an excellent example, were also distinguished by spreads of glitteringly bright quartz fragments concentrated in positions associated with the setting moon. There were deposits of human cremated bone at the centre of the ring.

Challengingly, these circles of the middle phase were the ancestors of others in SW Ireland. The latter were smaller and had the architecture and symbolism turned inside out: the biggest stones stand opposite a shrunken recumbent slab, and the alignment of the site is towards the sun rather than the moon. Such minute sites could never have accommodated more than a dozen people, and like their Scottish ancestral circles these rings must be regarded as the ritual centres of single families, rather than tribes, each erected on the land-holding of a few men and women

Drombeg was one of these well-planned monuments. Erected in the Middle Bronze Age, the final phase of stone circles, it is one of a medley of late rings. By 2000 BC stone circle customs were a mixture of movement, memory and mistake. An Irish recumbent stone circle was set up in the Channel Islands alongside an allée-couverte from Brittany. A Cornish ring was erected on Ile Beniguet near Ushant. Custom collapsed into a chaotic variety of shapes and size, some "rings" with four stones standing at the corners of a crude rectangle. These oddities, like Lundin Farm on its tree-grown mound, were first recognised in central Scotland, where they appear to be the warped descendants of the recumbent stone circles. Known as Four-Posters they have Irish cousins with a minuscule recumbent stone added to form a prosaically named Five-Stone ring; Kealkil in Co. Kerry is perhaps the best-known of these parochial settings in the south of Ireland.

Inside them, causing confusion to archaeologists, are the misleading burials left in them by people of later and different cults. The organic remains of skeletons and cremated bone produce radiocarbon dates that may be many years, perhaps even centuries, later than the actual use of the ring by its builders.

Although these terminal family "circles" may have been developed as places of intercession with the forces of nature, they were failures. Increasingly there was a deterioration in the weather, with rain waterlogging upland areas like Dartmoor and the Yorkshire Moors, conditions made worse by over-farming of thin soils, as on the denuded limestone terraces of the Burren in Co. Clare, once tilled and grazed in the Bronze Age, but now so bare that one of Cromwell's generals described it as having "Not a tree whereon to hang a man; no water in which to drown him; no soil in which to bury him." It is a manmade desert where gaunt wedge-tombs and portal-dolmens survive like skeletons of wanderers that had starved to death on the grassless land. Elsewhere, in Britain, Robert Louis Stevenson sensed similar desolation.

> Grey recumbent tombs of the dead in desert places,
> Standing-stones on the vacant wine-red moor,
> Hills of sheep, and the homes of the silent, vanished races,
> And winds, austere and pure.

By the Late Bronze Age stone circles were abandoned and left to decay. Their people departed. Only the stones remain for our curiosity. And it is because of their teasing questions about the mysteries of forgotten, irrecoverable rituals that had been performed in these empty rings that this book was conceived, illuminated by the imaginative camera of Max Milligan.

Artists and stone circles go together. Painters, poets and photographers see the rings not just as settings of upright stones but as circles of stones within a landscape of countryside and sky. John Keats knew it at Castlerigg near Keswick, "the gratification of seeing those aged stones, on a gentle rise in the midst of Mountains, which at that time darkened all round, except at the fresh opening of the Vale of St John". At Stonehenge, in *Don Juan*, Lord Byron despaired of his own ignorance.

> The Druid's groves have gone – so much the better.
> Stonehenge is not. But what the devil is it?

Another poet, Siegfried Sassoon, was more philosophical.

> What is Stonehenge? It is the roofless past;
> Man's ruinous myth; his uninterred adoring
> Of the unknown in sunrise cold and red;
> His quest of stars that arch his doomed exploring.
> And what is Time but shadows that were cast
> By these storm-sculptured stones while centuries fled?
> The stones remain; their stillness can outlast
> The skies of history hurrying overhead.

The weathered stones, the ruins, became symbols and visual images of present-day life and its decay as portrayed in two great paintings of Stonehenge. In 1835 John Constable made his "most ambitious" watercolour. Shrunken amidst the endless spaciousness of Salisbury Plain, Stonehenge lies under a cataclysmic sky whose turbulence is broken by a double rainbow that curves into the centre of the ring. Tiny figures stand motionless amongst the stones. Opposing this impression of permanence is a little running hare, a vanishing thing in a corner of the painting, a contrast between the transience of life and the enduring immobility of the stones.

Twenty years earlier Turner had a different vision. His *Stonehenge Sunset* is an exercise in artistic licence, the sarsens of the circle too thin, the lintels too many, to stress the angularity of the manmade monument. Like Constable's this is an apocalyptic scene. Hurled by a gale, rain pours down in a luminous light and the sky is turbulent with forked lightning. In the foreground, killed by the storm, lie the bodies of a shepherd and his sheep, statements of Christianity struck by the pagan forces of nature. A howling dog adds pathos to this image of death.

Whilst Constable's picture is more optimistic, both watercolours show how artists can discover truths and connections unsuspected by ordinary minds. Similarly, the patient, exploring eye of a photographer can catch comparable insights. There are impressions of fragility in stones that have lasted through rain-beaten, wind-gusted, snow-chilled centuries. The photographic eye captures the magic of light, whether in the Ring of Brodgar at sunset or in the prostrate slabs of Arbor Low, reclining like pallid sunbathers.

There is an awareness of stone itself: as at Callanish on Lewis with its contorted pillars lined with threads of quartz like filaments of fossilised silk. Another at Callanish becomes the half-finished statue of an Egyptian god.

An angle chosen for the photograph of a stone at Machrie Moor on Arran transforms it into the weatherworn profile of an Easter Island statue. There is humour. A cow at a ring on Machrie Moor uses its rump to provide a fifth boulder. A stony thumb of rock at Temple Wood in Argyllshire has an inelegant spiral near its knuckle. The blocks forming ring within ring at Yellowmead on Dartmoor stump from the ground like the studs of minutes on a gigantic clock. And the three remaining blobs of granite at the Spittal of Glenshee are reminiscent of little prions, "whale-birds", feeding on the back of a basking whale. It is imagination and awareness.

It is deceptive magic. The photographs illustrate and enlighten because they show not merely what can be seen but how they might have been seen by their makers who so frequently chose stones not just for their size and weight but often for their shape, their colour, for the fossil embedded in them, for the natural extrusions that resemble artificial cupmarks.

Stone circles are often called temples. But they are unlike today's church which is at the heart of its community. The church is a village history harbouring memorials, hatchments and armorial bearings. The church is Christianity against paganism. Stone circles are entirely different. They have no settlement. They are alone, empty, forgotten. What history they have died with their makers and we struggle to hear the faintest whispers of what people after them thought. Even early in their isolated desertion they fascinated. Romans were sightseers, to the Pyramids, to the Parthenon, to Stonehenge. Superstitious Saxons, Vikings and mediaeval peasants avoided stone circles for fear of the malignant spirits dwelling there. Clodagh, a Five-Stone ring in Co. Cork, was also known as Pookeen, "the place of fairies". The innocent-sounding name of Elva Plain near Keswick was a corruption of the Old Norse elf-haugr, "the mound of elves". As will be seen other place-names can be equally informative about past beliefs.

But for centuries there was no literature, and the first mention left to us came over two thousand years after the end of the circles when Henry, Archbishop of Huntingdon, in 1130 described Stonehenge as the Second Wonder of Britain "where stones of a wonderful size have been erected after the manner of doorways, so that doorway appears to have been raised upon doorway, nor can anyone conceive by what art such great stones have been so raised aloft, or why they were there erected". Two hundred years later similar questions were raised.

In the library of Corpus Christi College, Cambridge, is an early fourteenth-century manuscript. The scribe seems to have read Henry of Huntingdon.

His account also lists the Four Wonders of Britain and added to it is a brief reference to the splendid Rollright Stones in Oxfordshire. "In the Oxford country there are great stones, arranged as it were in some connection by the hand of man. But at what time this was done, or by what people, or for what memorial or significance, is unknown. Though by the inhabitants that place is called Rollendrith." The name tells us something of the way in which the ring was regarded, "the estate with special local rights belonging to Hrolla".

Such a place-name is historically informative. Others are simply depressing about the arithmetic of people living in the vicinity of a circle. Duddo Four Stones in Northumberland has five. Three Stone Burn at Ilderton still has thirteen in a ring from which some stones have been removed. There are Nine Maidens at the Merry Maidens, Boscawen-Un, Boskednan and Tregeseal, although all of those rings had nineteen or more stones. The Nine Stones at Belstone on Dartmoor, said to be petrified girls, has eleven closely set together, and once there may have been as many as forty. Adding mystery and hermaphroditic impossibility to innumeracy the ring is also known as the Seventeen Brothers.

Many other place-names were just as mundane, no more than rural descriptions of where or how the stone circle stood: Ballynoe, "the new town"; Auchquhorthies, "the field of stones"; Gors Fawr, "the great heath"; Aikey Brae, "the bank where oak trees grow"; the Standing Stones of Stenness, "the stones of the stones"; Drombeg, "the small ridge".

But Drombeg was also known as the Druid's Altar as if it was suspected that the ring had in some way been used for religion and ritual. There are similar instances. Pobull Fhinn, a splendid site on North Uist, was "the holy people". Reanscreena, a recumbent stone circle in Co. Cork, was "the ring of the shrine". Athgreany in the Wicklow Mountains was "the field of the sun" as though it was thought that the ring contained an ancient sightline. In the same way Beltany Tops, near Raphoe in Co. Donegal, got its name from the prehistoric festival of Beltane, a fire and solar occasion in May. Beltany Tops does have a good alignment towards the May Day sunrise. Tomnaverie, a recumbent stone circle in Aberdeenshire, was so called because it was "the hill of worship".

The name of the stone circle, avenue and short rows of Callanish on the island of Lewis in the Outer Hebrides has a convoluted history. Variously called *Callernish* and *Classerniss*, it has a suffix, Tursachen, "the stones of sadness or mourning". There has been an unscholarly attempt to convert these established forms of "Callanish" into a spurious Calanais, claiming this to be Celtic. It is not. It is Old Norse and comes from the Viking Kalladarnes, meaning "the promontory from which a ferry could be hailed". This was true. There is a very short stretch of water across Loch Roag from Callanish to Linshader. The interpretation is strengthened by the existence of another Callernish, a place on North Uist that looks across the narrow sound to Vallay Island.

Other place-names of rings are revelations of folk belief. The Merry Maidens in Cornwall and the Trippet Stones on Bodmin Moor in the same county are supposed to be girls turned to stone for dancing on the Sabbath and here place-names merge with local legends about the rings.

It is often assumed that folk stories about prehistoric monuments are no more than fairy tales that not only tell us nothing about our ancient past but are sometimes positive obstructions in our search for the truth. Yet there are examples of stories that have been remarkably informative about pre-Roman rituals and it is unlikely that these were made up by later people who misunderstood what the rings had been used for.

Where mediaeval people did manufacture explanations for the mysterious and colossal pillars they saw on their hillsides, they invented magical and anachronistic legends about the stones – that they had been raised by giants or King Arthur or Merlin, or even the Devil. These were commonsense solutions created by ignorant people who otherwise could not comprehend how such massive stones could ever have been put up. The very emphasis upon the Devil points to a Christian origin for these false explanations long after the circles had been deserted. It is likely that the names around Avebury in Wiltshire, the Devil's Den for a chambered tomb, the Devil's Brand-Irons for the Cove in Avebury's North Circle, the Devil's Quoits for the nearby Beckhampton Cove, were all titles given to the structures around the very time that the stones of the pagan rings were being toppled and buried by Christians in the early fourteenth century before the Black Death decimated men and beasts.

Legends of hidden treasure may be nothing more than wishful thinking, although it does seem odd that the round barrow at Rillaton, "the farm by the ford with a slab in it", on Bodmin Moor, close to the Hurlers stone circles, for years was reputed to be the home of a Druid whose spectre would give passers-by a drink from a gold cup. When this Bronze Age barrow was opened in 1818, as well as the expected bones and flints, the excavators actually found a lovely, ribbed vessel of thin, beaten gold. This may have been coincidence. Many other round barrows, supposedly concealing hoards of riches, have contained only cremations, pots and a few trinkets.

Yet one should perhaps remember the story of a now destroyed round cairn near Mold, *Bryn-yr-ellyllon*, "the hill of the goblins", which was said to be haunted by the golden ghost of a giant. Around 1810 when a wife was guiding her drunken husband across the field they were both startled to see "a figure of unusual size, clothed in a coat of gold which shone like the sun". Its appearance "scared the woman into fits and the man into sobriety". Over twenty years later when the cairn was excavated and levelled a tall skeleton was found in it with hundreds of precious amber beads and a gorgeous cape of gold which for a long time was displayed in the British Museum as a pony's breastplate. Folklore, or fakelore, such as this, however, tells us nothing about the practices that once took place inside the sacred enclosures of prehistoric people.

Nor do the associations with the Druids. These arose in the late seventeenth and early eighteenth centuries at a time when antiquarians such as the great field archaeologist John Aubrey realised that stone circles were older than Vikings, Saxons, Romans and early Christians because they existed in parts of Scotland and Ireland where those incomers had never been. Unfortunately, in Aubrey's time nothing was known of prehistoric Britain other than what writers like Julius Caesar had recorded at the very end of the Iron Age, a thousand or more years after the last ring had been abandoned.

In the absence of any deep knowledge of prehistory Aubrey and his colleagues had to make the reasonable assumption that it was the Druids, the priests and lawgivers mentioned by Caesar, who had ordered the erection of the stones. It is only since 1951 and the increasing refinement of radiocarbon determinations obtained from organic material that a better understanding of the lengths of time involved has developed. It has enabled archaeologists to date the megalithic structures to a period long before the Druids, far back in the remote past, five thousand years ago in the Neolithic and Bronze Ages of our islands.

It seems incredible that stories preserved by word of mouth alone could have lasted so long, enduring through two hundred generations, surviving the antagonisms of history and the hostility of evangelical Christians whose missionaries strove to expunge all traces of heathenism. Yet this may have happened in a few cases, and a deeper, more sympathetic approach to our folklore might reveal insights into antiquity that archaeology, with its dependence upon material remains, can never recapture.

At the thinnest, most wraithlike level of folk-memory there are the names of the rings, the Merry Maidens, Long Meg and Her Daughters, the Nine

Ladies, and the local beliefs that these are girls, always girls, turned into stone for dancing on the Sabbath. These too may be Christian myths but the legends of dancing and music and maidens are widespread from the Nine Maidens on Land's End up to Haltadans, the "Limping Dance" in the Shetlands, and right across to the Pipers' Stones in Co. Wicklow.

As rings of stones in other parts of the world were used for ritual dancing, it is arguable that the names of British rings preserve, like wisps, recollections of the activities that once took place inside them. It is noticeable that it is nearly always girls involved, never priests, and that sometimes it was a wedding party like the drunken revellers at Stanton Drew in Somerset that was petrified for the sin of dancing on the Sabbath, as though there were also memories of rites of fertility to ensure the fruitfulness of the land, acts of imitative magic that the Church would certainly have condemned as obscene and blasphemous.

Some stories are even more specific, involving a knowledge of geology or astronomy unlikely to be possessed, even by scholars, in mediaeval times. Stonehenge has been believed to be a good and well-known example. In his *History of the Kings of Britain*, *c.*1130–33 AD, Geoffrey of Monmouth explained how the sarsen uprights reached Salisbury Plain. "If you want to grace the burial place of these men with some lasting monument, replied Merlin, send for the Giant's Ring which is on Mount Killaurus in Ireland. In that place there is a stone construction which no man of this period could ever erect, unless he combined great skill and artistry. The stones are enormous and there is no one alive strong enough to move them." The bluestones at Stonehenge did come from the Preseli Mountains in SW Wales, the very region where prehistoric traders and copper prospectors landed on their journey from the gold-bearing mountains of the Wicklows in eastern Ireland to Salisbury Plain. It seemed hard to believe that Geoffrey of Monmouth arbitrarily selected the one correct direction for the transportation of the stones when he had the whole compass to choose from. Later Celtic myths tell of the same journey being taken so that there could have been an ancient literary source which Geoffrey himself would have come across.

Modern European people, accustomed to information being stored in books and files, are sometimes incredulous that oral myths and legends could be passed unchanged over many generations, but "primitive" societies would have found nothing improbable about this. Tom Harrison, in his *Savage Civilisation* of 1937 explained how natives in the Pacific islands of the New Hebrides, even though they learned easily enough, saw no need for reading and writing. "Cannot a man remember and speak?", they asked him, and Harrison commented that "words are a native art with an intricate circular pattern. The lay-out and content in the thousand myths which every child learns (often word-perfect, and one story may last for hours) are a whole library." It is only with the intrusion of literacy and urbanisation that such rote learning has been forsaken.

There is another mystery about Stonehenge. Geoffrey of Monmouth went on: "These stones are connected with certain secret religious rites and they have various properties which are medicinally important ... For they used to pour water over them. What is more, they mixed the water with herbal concoctions, and so healed their wounds. There is not a single stone among them which has not some medicinal virtue." Many stone circles – Avebury, Stanton Drew, Callanish amongst them – were linked by lines of earth or stones to water, and Stonehenge was no exception with its earth-banked avenue that curved down to the River Avon. Rites of purification may have taken place at the riverside but Geoffrey would not have perceived the connection between the circle and the river. By his time the weathered avenue was virtually undetectable, and the association could only have come to him through folk stories.

More remarkable still are the legends of astronomical events that had not been seen by any living person for centuries. In Ireland, not many miles north of Dublin, is the huge passage-tomb of Newgrange in Co. Meath, built around 3250 BC, with a long, stone-lined passage inside it leading to a beehive-shaped chamber with three side-cells where the burnt bones of the dead were laid. Over the centuries the mound of this passage-tomb became overgrown with weeds and a tumble of stones blocked the entrance. Yet an inexplicable story was told about this desolate shrine.

"A tradition had long existed that the rising sun, at some unspecified time, used to light up the three-spiral stone in the end-chamber of the tomb." This was impossible. The lintel over the entrance to the sloping passage was far too low for any sunlight to reach to the far end and the story was ignored as a piece of romantic nonsense. Then, during the excavations of 1962–75, Professor Michael O'Kelly of Cork University came across a feature unknown for five thousand years. Above the entrance, hidden under the collapse of cairn stones, was a thin rectangular opening, 6 feet long and 2 feet 6 inches high like a grossly exaggerated letterbox.

The preservation of this technically perfect astronomical device was fortunate. In 1874 Richard Burchett had attempted to remove the three-spiral "but two men with crowbars [were] incapable of moving it without greater risk to its safety than I was willing to incur . . . its mysteries remained unsolved" and did so until 21 December 1969, when O'Kelly stood in the chamber and watched the light of the sun penetrate the tomb at ten o'clock in the morning.

Once the roof-box had been cleared of its débris, the rays of the rising sun shone through its gap for just a few days at the midwinter solstice, the narrow beam penetrating the darkness and illuminating the end-cell with its carved slabs where the dead had rested. It shone directly onto three conjoined spirals carved on the eastern side-slab of the end-chamber. Significantly, the spirals were anti-clockwise, a pattern now known to be associated with midwinter, clockwise spirals being found in monuments linked with midsummer.

During the monument's use the entrance was blocked except when more bones were carried into the tomb, but when Midwinter's Day came, two quartz stones blocking the "roof-box" above it were pushed aside, allowing the sun to enter the passage and bring life to the cremated bones. Even when Newgrange was abandoned, the memory of this spectacular event survived thousands of years after the sun had last shone down the dark tunnel of the passage.

Surprisingly, Newgrange is not alone. Hundreds of miles to the north, on Orkney Mainland, is a similar passage-tomb, Maes Howe. Until the excavation of 1861, tumbles of stones accumulated in the passage, making access so difficult that the diggers found it easier to break into the chamber through the roof. Despite this there was a baffling legend about the place. "One of the astonishing stories they used to tell about Maeshowe was that at sunset on the winter solstice the sun for the only time shone through the long, low corridor and touched with light, fleetingly, the far wall of that chamber of death." George Mackay Brown, who recorded this, was able to test the tale easily because Maes Howe had been cleaned out and restored in the nineteenth century. On 21 December 1972 a group of people went there. The skies were clear and, sure enough, as the sun sank, red and dull, down to the horizon, "the sunset flowered on the stone – the last beam of light of the shortest day – and it glowed briefly on a wall that at every other time of the year is dark". It is largely unappreciated that, like Newgrange, Maes Howe had an astronomical "letterbox", this one formed by the huge rectangular slab that was used to block the SW-facing entrance. The stone was wide enough but not tall enough so that it left a gap above it where, because the passage of the tomb was angled, the setting November sun shone directly along it. This may have been intended as a warning that the winter solstice was approaching when the diffused light in the midwinter sunset would glow on the back slab of the tomb.

It is easy enough to understand why prehistoric people should have aligned their tombs, even their circles, on sunrise and sunset, why they should have associated the cold, gloomy midwinter with death, but it is only because legends about these beliefs have endured into modern times that excavators have been made aware of some of the almost forgotten rituals of these people.

Perhaps the most remarkable of all these little-known stories are those which are attached to the oddly named recumbent stone circles of NE Scotland. These peculiar rings such as Castle Fraser and Balquhain have a monstrous slab in their SW quadrant, lying flat between two tall pillars. Sometimes cupmarks (small depressions pecked and ground into the stone) are found on this recumbent and its flankers. Quartz was often scattered near them, and in the centre of the circle investigators have frequently discovered broken pottery, flints and human bones. Yet despite the prodigality of these finds the function of recumbent stone circles, as of all other megalithic rings, was notoriously hard to recover. Thankfully, folk stories have contributed much to our understanding of these sites which were put up by peasant families in the Late Neolithic and Early Bronze Ages, between about 3000 and 1800 BC, long before there was writing in Britain.

In the middle of the seventeenth century John Aubrey was writing to correspondents all over the kingdom, enquiring about the whereabouts of stone circles in their neighbourhood and asking what local fables there were about them. The Rev. James Garden, in a letter dated 15 June 1692, told Aubrey that there was a recumbent stone circle at Auchqhorthies, a few miles from Aberdeen, to which ancient priests were supposed to have forced people to carry "basketloads of earth which is given for the reason why this parcell of land (though surrounded with heath and moss on all sides) is better and more fertile than other places thereabout". Garden, despite his name, was no earth scientist. His report seemed ridiculous, but modern inspection of soil maps revealed an interesting pattern. Every one of the recumbent stone circles had been erected alongside a patch of fertile, well-drained and level land, avoiding steep slopes, scatters of rock and marshes, showing that their prehistoric builders had recognised these areas of good earth and had intentionally selected them for their circles. Without Garden's record of this local, half-remembered fact we might still be unaware of the expertise of these early farmers.

An even more fascinating, more esoteric glimpse of the past comes from another account of recumbent stone circles, written some two hundred years earlier. In his *History of Scotland*, published in 1527, Hector Boece mentioned these rings, of which there must have been over a hundred still standing in his time. In the early sixteenth century no one had any idea of the antiquity of these sites. Boece attributed them to a mythical Mainus, one of his thirty-nine Scottish kings. "In various localities of his territories . . . huge stones were assembled in a ring, and the biggest of them was stretched out on the south side (of the ring) to serve for an altar, whereon were burnt the victims in sacrifice to the gods." Completing this so-called fantasy, Boece added that the people also made a monthly offering inside the circles and "that is why the new moon was hailed with certain words of prayer, a custom which lingered very late".

This is an astonishing passage, containing as it does not only comments on the position of the recumbent stone – quite rightly reported to be towards the southern half of the circumference – but also a remark about cremations, of which nothing could have been known in the sixteenth century in the absence of any careful excavation. Still more striking is Boece's reference to the moon. Even the most modern researchers into the astronomy of these circles have said little about lunar alignments. Sir Norman Lockyer in the early twentieth century and Professor Alexander Thom, from the 1950s onwards, both noted for their investigations, found no consistent lunar rising or setting that could account for the slightly varying positions of the recumbent stones between SW and SSE, but knowing Boece's words it was possible for the present writer to solve the riddle.

The people who constructed these splendid rings seem to have regarded the moon as a symbol of life and death and they laid the recumbent stone in line with the southernmost moon, not as it rose or set, but between those positions as it moved across the night sky, shining down on the cupmarks and the white quartz and also onto the burnt bones at the centre of the ring. These bones were not the remains of burials. They were incomplete, there were too few bodies and too many of them were children such as the pitiful fragments of their broken skulls at Loanhead of Daviot. It is quite likely that these were offerings, even sacrifices, placed at the centre of the ring when it was first built by people whose need of protection from the malignant forces of nature was great and whose ceremonies were held at the time of the monthly full moon. They were concerned neither with the first sight of the moon nor with its last faint glow. Instead, they wished to see it in its full glory, high, brilliantly

lighting the night, so they aligned the recumbent stone anywhere between the moon's rising around the SSE and its setting at the SW in such a variety of alignments that they appeared meaningless to astronomers.

Without Boece we might never have recognised this. Without Garden and Geoffrey of Monmouth other mysteries might have remained unsolved. Sustained over lifetime after lifetime, these folk stories linger on, recollections of the past that too often still lie hidden in old, forgotten books.

Even in ruin a stone circle has stories to tell to the observant visitor. When one goes to a stone circle, whatever its condition, one travels through a tidy countryside of hedged fields where crops grow and cattle graze. It is a controlled land with farms, herds and flocks, metalled and signposted lanes, coppices and quarries. It is a mapped landscape, a manmade world. It is not prehistoric.

In those years, five millennia ago, there were few fields, few cattle, no sheep, no horses. It was an almost untouched landscape of uncontrolled rivers, miles of spreading trees, empty hillsides with animal tracks and tenuous ridgeway trails that avoided dangerous marshes, high above the sunless lostnesses of forests. It was a land of beasts and spirits. It was a world in which every thing, rock, brook, hill, cloud had life and was perceived by man in a way unreachable to the modern, western mind.

Today there are mere remnants. There are the pathless hills and mountains of Ardnamurchan, "the point of great sea", in western Scotland that juts twenty miles even farther to the west than Land's End. With its one winding, single-track road and steep cliffs above the long Loch Stannart its glens and mountains are almost as quiet as they were thousands of years ago. In western Ireland Connemara, "the Conmacne tribe of the sea", in Galway is a picturesque countryside, the lonely Partry Mountains, the beautiful pass between the Maamturks Mountains and the Twelve Bens with Lough Innagh at their foot, the innumerable loughs and pools and streams.

These are places of loveliness but they are also places of loneliness, they are desolation. Theirs is almost a prehistoric landscape but it is one that prehistoric man avoided. From the strange Five-Stone ring of Uragh in Co. Kerry there is a view across the valley to the mountainside and the waterfall and that is what man might have seen over three thousand years ago when the five tons of heavy outlier was being dragged up the hillside. The photograph traps it and offers a brief picture of the prehistoric eye.

Early Period Stone Circles

*c.*3200–2500 BC

Late Neolithic to Early Bronze Age

The first stone circles were phenomena of the Late Neolithic or New Stone Age period. Where or why the first was built is unclear. It was once thought that the rings had been constructed by Beaker people during the Early Bronze Age, but in reality many of the largest and most imposing rings were raised by native farming communities long before Beaker people came to Britain.

If the earliest were megalithic imitations of henges, earthen enclosures of eastern Britain, then it is not surprising that the rings of stone reflected that ancestry in their shape and size. Concentrated around the coasts of the Irish Sea and the sea routes of the Atlantic from Ireland to Scotland, circles such as Castlerigg in Cumbria and the Ring of Brodgar on the Orkneys were few but impressive. They were large, of many stones, usually over 100 feet in diameter, and were true circles.

There were others in north-eastern Scotland. Known as recumbent stone circles because of the long, prostrate block at their SW, sites such as Loanhead of Daviot were probably Irish in origin. Until recently they were believed to be Bronze Age monuments but this has been disproved. With their tall pillars, carvings, scatters of white quartz and subtle alignments on the southern moon they are some of the finest and most challenging of all stone circles.

a burial-chamber, at its centre. A congregation of no more than two hundred participants might be imagined.

The blocks of the Cove are now prostrate, two huge sides tumbled outwards, a long low stone on edge like a sill or doorstep between them at the east, and other little stones nearby. The corpse of a stockily built man was buried against the eastern corner. Just to the east was a deep pit with a human armbone in it. "It is possible", wrote the excavator Harold St George Gray, "that a skeleton or skeletons may have been removed from here".

The connection with death is manifest at Arbor Low, suggesting funerary rites and rituals of fertility. The Cove may have been planned to face the major northern moonrise to the NE. It is quite possible that the very first structure here, standing remote and gaunt on its hillside, was the focus of burial rites at a time when stone circles were unknown.

Later prehistoric people dug out stretches of the bank against the eastern side of the SSE entrance to raise a big round barrow in which human bones, flints and two Early Bronze Age food vessels were found. What appears to be the beginnings of an earthen avenue curves away from the entrance, turning towards the mound of Gib Hill 330 yards west of Arbor Low.

It has been claimed that no fewer than fifty straight ley-lines intersected at Arbor Low. More persuasively it appears that this circle-henge was the sub-tribal focus of a well-populated countryside, usurping the roles of earlier family shrines. It lies at the heart of a landscape of eight Early Neolithic chambered tombs. In turn it became the centre of dozens of Bronze Age cairns. It is one of the wonders of megalithic Britain.

Other places of interest. The denuded circle-henge of the Bull Ring, SK 078 783, is 10 miles NW. The exposed slabs of the Five Wells chambered cairn, SK 124 710, are 5 miles NNW.

The leaning pillar betrays the fact that the stones once stood upright

2

Ballynoe
Co. Down

J 481 404

2¹/₂ miles south of Downpatrick

Dawn mist surrounds the Ballynoe Circle
with the mountains of Mourne on the
horizon beyond

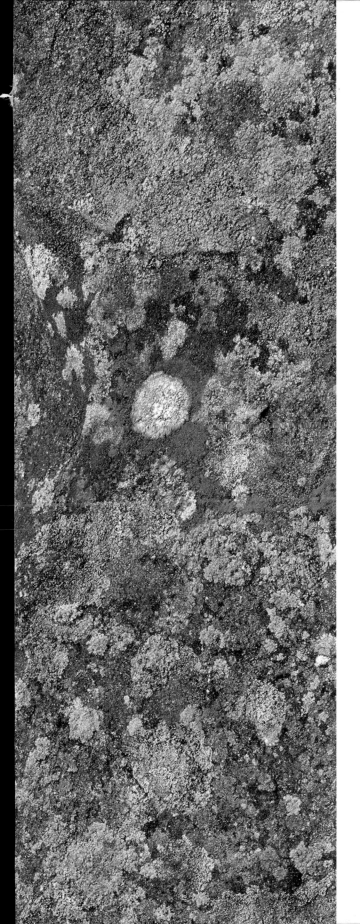

The large and impressive circle of Ballynoe, "the new settlement", lies on low, fertile ground. With its Cumbrian traits of close-set stones, alignments and an entrance, it consists of over fifty close-set uprights, up to 6 feet high, enclosing a space about 110 feet across. Two western pillars stand 7 feet apart outside the circle, forming a portalled entrance. There are also four outlying stones, two to the NE, two to the SW, but they may be no more than casual erratics, as they have neither a directional nor an astronomical significance.

Inside the circle is a long, kerbed sub-rectangular mound lying east–west. It was excavated in 1937–8 and was the last of two periods of interference with what was once a fine open stone circle.

Immediately inside the ring on the west is an arc of six stones against the edge of the mound. They are the dismantled remains of two kerbed, round cairns that had been put up inside the circle. They had a short life. The vaguely oblong mound was built over them, using many of their kerbstones for its own. The 5-foot-high mound had large cists at its ends. Both contained cremated bones, but the only pottery recovered was a decorated rim sherd of Late Neolithic ware. Between the cairn and kerb, set in the ground, were some smooth boulders known as baetyls or sacred stones associated with burials.

Ballynoe has kept its mutilated secrets. In the beginning it was a counterpart to Swinside in the Lake District, circular, of many closely set stones, with a portalled entrance aligned on the setting of the sun halfway between midwinter and midsummer. Only prehistoric bigotry and vandalism ruined this magnificent monument.

Other places of interest. Castle Mahon stone circle, J 552 470, is 5 miles NE. Legananny portal-dolmen, J 289 434, is 7 miles WNW. Audleystown dual-court tomb, J 561 505, is 6 miles NE.

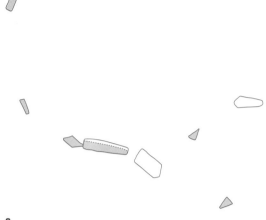

3
Balquhain
Aberdeenshire

NJ 735 241
Three miles NW of Inverurie

This damaged recumbent stone circle on a hillside has several interesting features. It is sometimes known as the Chapel of Garioch from the Kirk a mile to the west.

The local stones, on the circumference of a circle 68 feet across, are a variety of red granite, quartzite and basalt, but the recumbent stone, which is 12 feet 6 inches long and weighs over 10 tons, is a white-grained granite which came from some distance away.

Originally there were probably twelve stones in the ring. An impressive outlier of quartz, over 10 feet tall, stands just to the SE. The fallen east flanker has several cupmarks on it. The stone to the west of the west flanker has two conspicuous groups of cupmarks on its outer surface. There is a possible cupmark on the upper surface of the recumbent stone. All three of these decorated slabs were placed in important positions of the moon.

A limited excavation in 1900 uncovered a rough pavement of boulders under the earth, perhaps the remains of a ring-cairn in which human cremated bones were buried.

Other places of interest. Loanhead of Daviot stone circle, NJ 747 288, is 3 miles NNE (see No.8 below). Easter Aquorthies circle, NJ 732 208, is 2 miles south. There is an interesting museum above the library in Inverurie 2³/₄ miles SE.

The Plough constellation moves over the quartz outlier under the light of the full moon

4

Beltany Tops
Co. Donegal

C 254 003

Two miles south of Raphoe

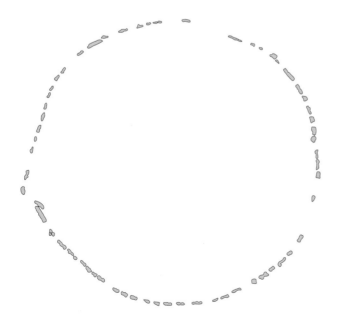

Circles of Stone

Known as Beltany or Tops stone circle, this unusual monument on an isolated hilltop should properly be classed as a late outlier of the Carrowmore cemetery seventy miles to the SW. Its most impressive feature is the orthostatic kerb, which is an early form of stone circle.

It consists of over sixty stones averaging 4 feet in height. Some are contiguous; others are separated by large boulders. There is no break in the circle, which has a diameter of 145 feet. In two places, at the east and the west, two pillars are very tall and well-shaped, reaching the imposing height of 9 feet. A single stone 6 feet high stands 70 feet outside the ring to the SE. A 4-foot-high churned-up pile of boulders occupies the interior like a pillaged cairn. This and the close-standing boulders link Beltany to the Carrowmore boulder-circles.

The inner face of a triangular slab at the ENE is covered in cupmarks. From the high pillar at the WSW the decorated stone marks the place of the May Day sunrise. Unsurprisingly, the date was that of the prehistoric festival of Beltane, "the shining one", whose celebration is commemorated in the name of this misunderstood ring.

Other places of interest. Grianan of Ailoch hillfort, C 336 197, is 14 miles NNE. Mevagh cup-and-ring-marked rock, C 121 397, is 18 miles NNW.

5
Carrowmore
Co. Sligo

G 663 335
Two miles SW of Sligo

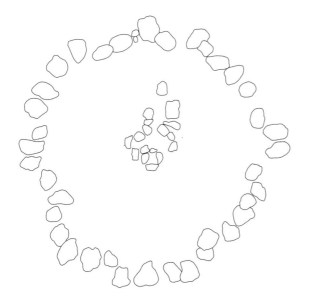

In the far west of Ireland, Carrowmore, "the spacious quarter", is a widespread but savagely ruined chambered cairn-cemetery, extending over an area about a mile long by half a mile wide. It is a landscape of low hills on a limestone plain. To the west is the jagged mountain of Knocknarea, "the royal hill", on whose top rises the gigantic Maeve's Cairn, the burialplace of the Celtic goddess.

Once of some two hundred sites, today only sixty can now be seen. Many of the tombs had cairns set inside a boulder kerb, the trademark of the complex because they were the ancestors of true stone circles. Except for one at the very heart of the necropolis there are few genuine megalithic tombs. Most are unroofed boulder-circles, wide rings of closely set big boulders surrounding a low, flat-topped cairn. Inside other boulder-circles is a dolmen with a capstone. Significantly the majority have no trace of a central structure.

At Carrowmore there was a steady development from passage-tomb to boulder-circle to stone circle. The photograph shows further change. A boulder-circle at the far NE of the cemetery and in the town of Sligo itself was first depaganised by the addition of Christian icons and then urbanised by becoming a traffic-island. Few prehistoric ritual monuments have been so transformed.

Four of the Carrowmore sites were excavated between 1977 and 1979, proving to be very early burialplaces of immigrant farming families. From such uncomplicated monuments, their central burials spiritually protected by a ring of contiguous boulders separating the dead from the profane world, gradually developed the idea of an open stone circle.

All four were boulder-circles and none had the passage of the classic Irish passage-tomb. Radiocarbon dates from three sites averaged 3043 bc, in real years some time between 3900 BC and 3650 BC; either date is very early for stone circles in Britain and Ireland.

At Carrowmore there is a line of increasingly spaced monuments extending to the NNE by the end of which the sites had become true stone circles. Site 57 was a large free-standing ring of thirty-three heavy boulders weighing 4 to 5 tons each. It would have taken perhaps a score of workers to move them into position.

Almost at the end of the cemetery is another spacious ring, here with only five remaining stones. It is noticeable that the farther these open rings are from the central passage-tomb, the less closely set are their stones and the bigger the rings become – the wide, open space for the open-air rituals of people who had abandoned all memories of the darkness of a chambered tomb. They were the beginnings of recognisable stone circles.

Other places of interest. Carrowkeel passage-tomb cemetery, G 755 115, is 15 miles SSE. Deerpark central-court tomb, G 753 367, is 6 miles ENE. Creevykeel full-court tomb, G 721 546, is 13 miles NNE.

A frosted dawn highlights ancient plough
trails surrounding the ring

6
Castlerigg
Cumberland

NY 292 236

1¹/₂ miles east of Keswick

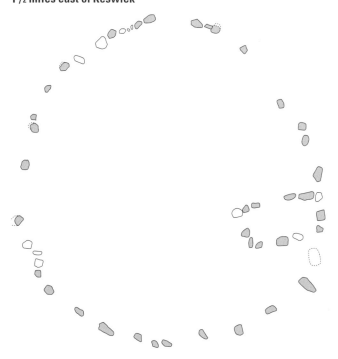

On Chestnut Hill on level ground alongside a lane from Keswick is one of the most evocative rings in Britain. It is spectacularly situated amongst the surrounding mountains and has the further distinction of being probably one of the earliest stone circles, constructed around 3200 BC, towards the end of the Neolithic period. This was a time when the Lake District, at whose heart it stands, was at its busiest and most important, because of the busy production of stone axes in the Langdale Mountains a few miles to the south. It is likely that one function of the circle was to act as a depôt for the distribution of the tools into southern England and Scotland.

The stones are all local slate, standing anything from 3 feet to 7 feet 6 inches high. The largest and heaviest, on the south-eastern arc of the ring, weighs around 16 tons. A team of at least seventy workers would have been needed to set it upright. Unusually the great stone was arranged to stand at right angles to the circumference, like a playing-card standing edge on.

In the beginning there were about forty-two blocks in the ring, which is not a perfect circle but flattened at its NE so that the diameters vary from 107 to 97 feet. There is a noticeably wide entrance at the exact north formed by two tall blocks whose size and height is emphasised by the much smaller stones on either side of them. There are the faintest traces of an outer bank, and a discerning eye can make out the circular outlines of three or four robbed cairns inside the ring, intrusive burialplaces set up in the Bronze Age, when the ring had lapsed into disuse. In turn those cairns were removed when some stones of the circle were removed to allow ploughs to be taken into the ring's interior and crops to be planted.

An outlying stone almost a hundred yards away to the WSW, standing by a hedge, may have been one of those uprooted circle-stones. Perhaps just to get it out of the way it was buried close to the ring, but its pit was too shallow and plough-shares scraped along it, damaging them and scoring deep lines across its upper surface. Re-excavated, it was dumped at the side of the field and used as a stile until put upright around 1913. Suggestions that it had been a prehistoric astronomical outlier to mark the early November sunset were mistaken.

An enduring question about Castlerigg is the presence of a unique rectangle of low stones, about 22 feet long and 11 feet wide, inside the ring at the SE. It is aligned ESE–WNW and has no known astronomical purpose. An excavation in 1882 found nothing except a small pit at the western end with only charcoal mixed with the earth.

Unlike the so-called outlier at the WSW, the tall pillar at the SE did have an astronomical purpose and this explains its side-on situation. Looking from the centre of the ring in early February, the prehistoric festival of Imbolc (now the Christian Candlemas), an observer would have seen the sun rising between the high fells of Matterdale Common three miles to the SE.

Unusually, no legends attach to this grandiose ring. It has been said that its local name is the "Carles", as though the stones were husbandmen turned into stone for some forgotten sin, but the name is wrong. It was a mistaken reading of "Caréles", written by the antiquarian, William Stukeley, in the early eighteenth century: "They call it the caréles, and corruptly, I suppose, Castle-rigg". Otherwise folk-stories have ignored the stones.

Other places of interest. The disturbed stone circle of Elva Plain lies on farmland at NY 176 317, 9 miles NW. The probably spurious but attractive Blakeley Raise lies close to a road at NY 060 140, 15 miles SW.

7

Druids' Circle &
Circle 275
Gwynedd

SH 722 746

Four miles WSW of Conway

SH 745 747

250 yards ENE of the Druids' Circle

A view to Llandudno across Conway Bay

This well-known circle stands on the headland of Penmaenmawr, proudly over-looking Conway Bay at a height of 1310 feet O.D. Half a mile NNW is the Neolithic axe factory of Graig Lwyd. The ring was built alongside a prehistoric trackway.

Some thirty local granite stones stand, unevenly spaced, in a low rubbly bank with an entrance marked by taller stones at the WSW. The oval ring measures about 84 feet by 80 feet. Excavation in 1958 discovered a central scatter of stones covering two burials, one the cremation of a child beneath an enlarged food vessel in a small cist, the second the cremation of another child. Another food vessel, a small bronze knife and three whetstones were also found.

It is dangerous to swear near the judgmental Deity Stone at the south. Opposite is the Stone of Sacrifice. Any baby less than a month old laid briefly on its ledge would have everlasting good luck.

A little ring, some 250 yards ENE of the Druids' Circle, stands on a slight slope. Known as Circle 275 it was completely excavated in 1959. Little could better demonstrate the lack of poetry amongst archaeologists than that this charming ring should be given a prosaic number rather than a name that would inform visitors of its distant origins. Lying on the hillside of Penmaenmawr it is usually ignored by people heading towards the famous Druids' Circle a few yards ahead at the crest of the rise. The little ring merits attention.

Although it was completely excavated in 1959, its ancestry was not recognised until some thirty years later. It is tiny. Five rounded but low boulders surround an open interior about 10 feet across. There is a suspicion of a bank of small stones between the stones at the south. Inside the ring masses of local quartz fragments had been strewn, and in a central pit there was more quartz. Significantly, the lowest but heaviest of the low boulders is at the SW and this is the clue to its inspiration. It is a recognisable version of the Five-Stone recumbent stone circles of SW Ireland, of which Kealkil (No.57), Knocknakilla (No.58) and Uragh (No.68) in this book are examples.

It may be assumed that its presence so far from its homeland was the result of traders in Irish copper ores bringing the material to north Wales and setting up their own small shrine.

Other places of interest. Graig Lwyd axe-factory site, SH 717 750, is 1 mile NW. The Cors y Carneddau cairns, SH 716 747, are 1 mile west. Cerrig Pryfaid stone circle, SH 724 713, is 2¼ miles south.

In dawn light, the Druids' Circle lies on the horizon above Circle 275

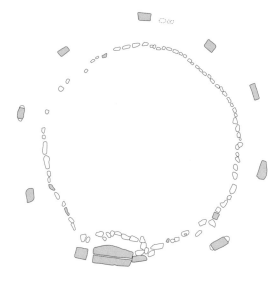

8

Loanhead of Daviot
Aberdeenshire

NJ 747 288
Five miles NNW of Inverurie

This recumbent stone circle stands on a gentle slope into which a levelled platform was cut. A long plantation of dark trees obscures the view to the south. The ring is 67 feet in diameter.

The recumbent, split by frost, is flanked by two tallish stones from which, typically, the other circle stones decline in height. Each stone stood in a little cairn beneath which there was a pit with charcoal and flat-rimmed ware. Characteristically, the recumbent stone at the SSW lay in line with the major southern moonset. A vertical line of twelve cupmarks is carved on the inner face of the stone standing to the east of the east flanker. From the centre of the ring the decorated stone is aligned on the midwinter sunset.

Inside the ring is a disturbed ring-cairn with an open central space. Excavation in 1932 revealed that a pyre of willow branches had blazed inside the circle before the ring-cairn was raised. Sherds, charcoal and human cremated bone, including skull fragments of children two to four years of age, rested in the central space, with flint scrapers and knives.

Immediately east of the circle are the much-damaged remains of an enclosed cremation cemetery from which Bronze Age food-vessel urns and human cremations have been recovered. In the stone circle the discovery of native Lyles Hill ware and some early beaker sherds in positions later than the construction of the ring suggest that it may have been erected in the years around 3000 BC. It is likely that the enclosed cremation cemetery was constructed when the circle was falling into disuse.

Opposite: The cremation cemetery with the circle beyond

Other places of interest. In the woods just to the SE of the circle are two outcrops with two cupmarks on them. New Craig recumbent stone circle, NJ 745 296, is ¹/₂ mile north. There is a report that a third recumbent stone circle was destroyed when Daviot church, ¹/₂ mile SE, was built around 1825 (see also Balquhain, No.3).

Opposite: The only recumbent stone, possibly split by prehistoric ice

9

Long Meg and Her Daughters
Cumberland

NY 571 373

2¹/₄ **miles north of Langwathby**

Perplexingly built on a slope, this is one of the largest British rings, about 359 feet by 305 feet in diameter. It is in state care.

Some seventy local porphyritic stones remain of a ring flattened at the north, where aerial photography showed the outline of a vast enclosure against which the ring was erected, explaining the circle's strange situation. Two massive blocks stand almost exactly east and west of the circumference. There are traces of a bank, perhaps no more than upcast from ploughing, at the WSW. Two enormous boulders define a wide entrance at the SW, with two more beyond them as portals.

Thirty yards beyond them stands Long Meg, a scrawnily thin red sandstone pillar, possibly brought from the Eden Valley a mile and a half away. Its eastern side has several carvings of rings and anti-clockwise spirals on it. They have been interpreted as representations of the sun's winter path, and it is true that from the circle Long Meg does indicate the position of the midwinter sunset.

John Aubrey reported that two large cairns stood at the centre of the ring. William Stukeley noticed their remains in 1725 but they have now gone, eradicated by the planting of crops in the eighteenth and nineteenth centuries.

There are legends. The stones cannot be counted. Believed to be the petrified bodies of Long Meg, a witch, and her offspring, it was said that if a piece was broken off Long Meg, she would bleed.

Other places of interest. A little cairn-circle of huge blocks, Little Meg, in the field ¹/₂ mile WNW, NY 576 374, was thought by Alexander Thom to lie in line with the May Day sunrise. Glassonby cairn-circle is 1¹/₂ miles north at NY 575 393.

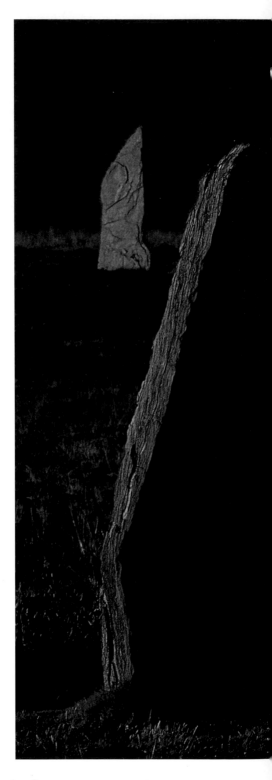

10

Ring of Brodgar
Orkney Mainland

HY 294 133
Four miles NE of Stromness

This magnificent circle-henge stands on a low-lying neck of land between the lochs of Harray and Stenness. It is one of the largest circles in Britain and Ireland.

The ring of stones stands on a plateau sloping down to the east, surrounded by a rock-cut ditch. There are wide entrances at the NW and SE but no trace of an outer bank. Inside the ditch a circle of tall sandstone slabs was erected, the stones perhaps coming from an outcrop half a mile to the north at Bookan. There may originally have been up to sixty. They are all spectacular slabs, the tallest l8 feet 6 inches high, but today many have gone and the most impressive arc is between the NW and SE.

Some yards to the SE on a low, circular platform, is a squat monolith known as the Comet Stone. The stumps of two others stand near it, perhaps the remains of a Cove such as once existed inside the nearby Standing Stones of Stenness.

A stone axe and flint leaf-shaped arrowhead were found inside the circle, which is surrounded by round cairns, presumably of the Bronze Age and later than the circle-henge which may have been erected around 2800 BC.

Brodgar, close to the Comet Stone, was formerly known as the Temple of the Sun because of its complete circle. The incomplete crescent of the Stones of Stenness was the Temple of the Moon. In 1851 the antiquarian F. W. L. Thomas was dismissive of this celestial landscaping. Referring to the tumbled Ring of Bookan a mile to the NW

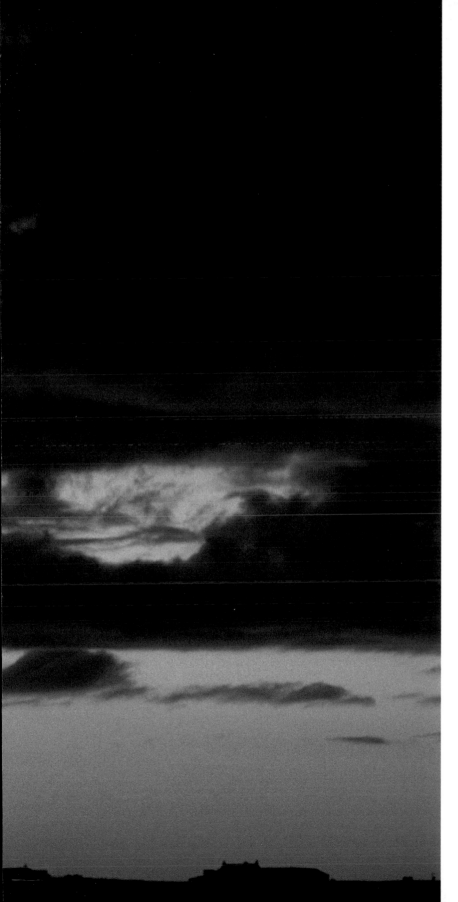

Erosion by frost has carved a "face" reminiscent of those on Easter Island

On midsummer nights it never gets completely dark in Orkney

he observed, "Unfortunately the Ring of Bukan, which was, of course, the Temple of the Stars, seems to have escaped notice, or we might have learned of some more ante-nuptial ceremonies performed therein." Alexander Thom, who was convinced of Brodgar's astronomical associations, was impressed by the design and positioning of the ring. "The Brogar site is the most perfect example of a megalithic lunar observatory that we have left in Britain. The ring and ditch were probably placed on this little hill at first because from here there are four foresights marking the approximate position of the rising/setting moon at the major and minor stand-stills. Perhaps about a thousand years later

the accurate observatory was built from a cairn of earth, built with such accuracy that we can today date the observatory by the slowly changing obliquity of the ecliptic to about 1600 B.C. Large mounds were built so that watchers could be placed on the top to warn the people below of the impending rising of the moon."

Other places of interest. The Stenness circle-henge, HY 306 125, is ³/₄ mile to the SE. Maes Howe passage-tomb, HY 317 127, is 1¹/₂ miles ESE. Unstan stalled cairn, HY 282 117, is 1¹/₄ miles SW.

This famous ring, whose name may derive from *Hrolla-landriht*, "the land with special local rights belonging to Rolla", stands on a high ridge. Its local pillars of corroded limestone have somewhat smoother inner faces and may have been dressed. The ring once consisted of about a hundred stones shoulder to shoulder, but it is difficult to assess the original number because many have broken through weathering, and stumps and tops and fragments are intermingled around the circumference. Many were removed in the nineteenth century and replaced in 1882. The circle measures 108 feet in diameter. It has a disturbed portalled entrance at the SE, aligned on the major southern moonrise.

Eighty-four yards NNE is the outlying King Stone, 8 feet high. Almost a quarter of a mile to the east is the denuded portal dolmen of the Whispering Knights, in which a human jawbone was found. In an earlier

11

Rollright Stones
Oxfordshire

SP 296 308

2¹/₄ miles NW of Chipping Norton

Opposite: The King Stone sits in the top left corner

excavation Ralph Sheldon, a seventeenth-century antiquarian, dug for bones at the centre of the ring. He was unsuccessful.

The Rollright Stones is a "Cumbrian" stone circle, as its closely set stones, circularity, size, and entrance show. Erected around 3000 BC, one of its functions may have been to act as a staging post for the distribution of Lake District stone axes to the heavily populated regions of southern England. Legends of witchcraft and of warriors turned to stone are attached to this ring.

Other places of interest. Lyneham chambered tomb, SP 297 211, is 6 miles south. Lyneham Camp hillfort, SP 299 214, is 6 miles south. Chastleton Camp plateau fort, SP 259 283, is 3¹/₂ miles SW.

The stones are "corroded like worm-eaten wood, by the harsh jaws of time" wrote William Stukeley in the early eighteenth century

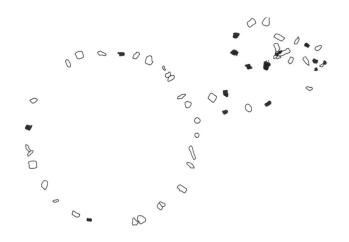

12

Stanton Drew
Somerset

ST 603 630

Six miles south of Bristol

Stanton Drew has nothing to do with druids. The name means "the homestead with stones belonging to the Drew or Drogo family". Long before the early mediaeval period when the family owned the land, three stone circles were put up near the River Chew. The undressed stones were mostly local silicious breccia, but some are oolitic limestone, possibly from Dundry Hill four miles NW.

The rings lie on a bent NE–SSW axis. The NE ring, once of eight stones, measures 97 feet across; the central, which is the largest of all megalithic rings except for Avebury, about 376 feet. It had some 32 stones. The SSW ring, ruined but 145 feet in diameter, had twelve stones. All the stones are large and coarsely roughened.

There is an interesting repetition of multiples of four in the numbers of stones and in the unit of measurement, 3 feet $^1/_2$ inch, used in their layout, about 124 for the central ring, 32 and 48 for the others.

Over a quarter of a mile to the NE the stump of an outlying stone, Hautville's Quoit, lies by the hedge of a field on a ridge overlooking the circles. Beyond St Mary's church to the SW of the rings are the three slabs of a Cove. The wreckage of two avenues extends from both the north-eastern and central circles. The complex, with its Cove, avenues, multiple rings and outlying stone, has close affinities with Avebury, thirty miles to the east.

John Aubrey was told that the stones were the bodies of a wedding party petrified for continuing to dance into the Sabbath. The avenues were the fiddlers. Behind the church the slabs of the Cove were the tall standing groom and his shorter bride facing him; the drunken parson lay flat on his back between them.

Other places of interest. Chambered tombs lie within a few miles of Stanton Drew but all are severely damaged. The Priddy henges, ST 540 527, are 5 miles south.

A gale blows up 3-foot waves on the usually calm loch of Stenness

13

Standing Stones of Stenness
Orkney

HY 306 125

Four miles NE of Stromness

Excavated in 1973–4 Stenness, "the stones", is a circle-henge with a single entrance. Some 130,000 tons of hard rock were quarried from the wide, 6-foot-deep ditch, an incredible 40,000 man-hours of toil with wedges, antler picks and human muscles in the years around 3000 BC.

The bank has been worn down by weather and is inconspicuous. Inside it was the stone circle 104 feet in diameter, once of twelve local sandstones. Only three superb sandstone slabs still stand, the tallest 18 feet 9 inches high, at the south opposite the northern entrance. A fourth is broken to about half its original height. Four others were discovered and the stoneholes of three more. Only the existence of the twelfth stone is uncertain, where a gap at the SE coincided with the place of midwinter sunrise. Inside the ring is a cove. Four slabs at the ring's centre form a rectangular setting, perhaps a representation of the hearths found at Skara Brae.

Other places of interest. Stenness has outliers. One, the Watch Stone, 18 feet 6 inches high, stands to the north at the narrowest point of the isthmus and may once have been part of an avenue. Another stone, the holed Odin Stone or the "Stone of Sacrifice", stood 150 yards north of Stenness. It was destroyed in 1814 by the landowner despite its being considered a place of betrothal for young islanders. Ernest Marwick recorded how young lovers held hands through the hole. "The Odin oath was so binding that a Stromness woman who had sworn it with her pirate sweetheart [John Gow, executed in 1725] travelled to London, after he was hanged in chains off Greenwich, and retracted it as she held his dead hand."

14

Swinside
Cumberland

SD 171 882

Five miles north of Millom

Swinside, "the hillside on which pigs graze", is a marvellous ring. It is also known as Sunkenkirk, because the Devil was believed to have pulled the stones of a new church into the ground each night until its builders despaired of finishing it, leaving the stark foundations for visitors to marvel at today.

This lovely ring stands in an amphitheatre of hills and mountains at the SW corner of the Lake District, where its remoteness has preserved it from the damage that many stone circles have suffered because of their nearness to farms and villages. Only one or two stones have been taken away to leave gaps that allowed ploughs into the centre. Otherwise the circle is perfect.

Five thousand years ago about sixty grey stones were dragged from the nearby fells to be set up in a true circle, 93 feet 8 inches in diameter, standing closely together as though in need of each other's company. The tallest, an elegantly lithe pillar, tapering to a point, is 7 feet 6 inches high and is almost exactly at the north of the site, a little to the NNE. It looks across the circle to a stone that is its opposite in every respect, squat, broad and flat-topped, set sturdily at the south. It has been interpreted as the "female" counterpart to its phallic partner on the other side of the ring. Such fertility symbolism is suspected at other early rings. There is nothing ordinary about Swinside. As well as the north and south stones there is also an obviously designed entrance at the SE, where two extra stones have been placed as portals just outside the circumference. There is a subtlety. An alignment from the centre of Swinside across the

tops of the two south blocks of the entrance – the circle stone and the portal beyond it – has a compass-bearing of 134°.5 which looks towards the distant hillside and the place where the midwinter sun would rise at the dark end of the year. A similar arrangement exists at Long Meg and Her Daughters near Penrith.

It would have taken at least fifty workers a month to bring the stones from the hillsides, dig their holes and erect them, creating an open space where a hundred or more people assembled at the bleakest, emptiest part of the year. Only imagination can tell us what ceremonies they performed, what their fears were. No more than the stones survive.

Other places of interest. The stone circle is not isolated. 4³/₄ miles SSW at SW 150 814 are the three little rings and short stone row of Lacra. A fine pair of standing stones can be seen 5 miles SSW at "The Giant's Grave", Kirksanton, SD 135 810.

Middle Period Stone Circles

***c.*2500–2000 BC**

Early Bronze Age

The time when metallurgy began in Britain and Ireland and when beaker pottery and the mysterious vessels known as Grooved Ware were being deposited inside ritual monuments was also the time when many of the most perfect rings were built, delights such as Boscawen-Un in Cornwall and, in the Outer Hebrides, Callanish on the Isle of Lewis and the delicacy of Loch Buie on Mull. They could be circular or oval, the latter usually having a long axis in line with a solar or lunar event, and they could be grotesque distortions like the travesties of circularity at Beaghmore in northern Ireland. Unexpectedly at such an early time for prehistoric people it is also becoming clear that there were preferred numbers of stones from region to region, evidence of numeracy amongst these early societies.

The practice of putting up megalithic rings was taken up widely in Britain and Ireland until almost everywhere where there was fertile land and outcrops of rock there were stone circles. Whether in the Wicklow Mountains of eastern Ireland, or in the glens and on the hillsides of central Scotland, or on the granite uplands of Bodmin Moor and Land's End there was an outburst of stone circle building, smaller rings than those of the earlier period, often around 60 feet across and presumably for groups of neighbouring families, who would assemble there at chosen times of the year. There were always exceptions. Colossal enclosures like Avebury must have been settlement, fortification and ritual enclosure combined, a contradiction proving that there are few blueprints to be imposed on the continuing mysteries of stone circles.

15
Athgreany
Co. Wicklow

N 930 032
1½ miles south of Hollywood

Athgreany is the corrupt form of *Achadh greine*, "the field of the sun". The ring is splendidly preserved, probably the finest of the stone circles in the Wicklow Mountains, on whose rocky slopes prehistoric prospectors searched for nuggets of gold.

The ring is yet another Pipers' Stones in which dancers had been petrified. It is perfectly circular, 75 feet 6 inches in diameter and perhaps originally of twenty-four ungraded stones placed on a hill-terrace. As in the circle-henge of Boleycarrigeen to the south, the taller stones are on either side of an eastern gap, making it likely that this was intended as an entrance. Two gnarled trees interrupt its circumference.

To the NE a prostrate avocado-shaped boulder may be a glacial erratic rather than a fallen outlier. If erect it would point the expectant eye to a nearby hillside in which there is a saddle at about 48°, an azimuth in line with the midsummer sunrise. The phenomenon may account for the name, just as Beltany in Co. Donegal seems to be a memory of Beltane and the May Day sunrise.

Other places of interest. Boleycarrigeen stone circle, N 938 892, is 8½ miles south. Punchestown standing stone, N 918 165, is 8 miles NNW. Curragh henges, N 780 130, are 12 miles WNW. Moylisha wedge-tomb, NS 930 675, is 22 miles south.

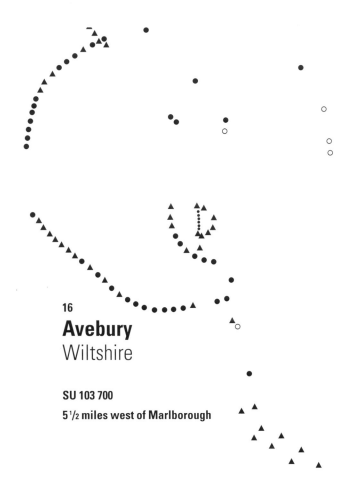

16
Avebury
Wiltshire

SU 103 700

5 ¹/₂ miles west of Marlborough

Avebury is a gargantuan astonishment. Everything about it is outsize. Near it is the largest long barrow, the largest causewayed enclosure, the tallest manmade mound. It is the Texas of prehistory.

Its outer bank is high and a quarter of a mile across. Inside it an upright telegraph pole could have been hidden in its ditch. Along its edge is the widest stone circle in Britain, Ireland and Brittany, the stones at its four entrances the slabbiest and heaviest of all the rings. It surrounds the sad remnants of the south circle, another vast ring, where a central sarsen stood until eighteenth-century entrepreneurs toppled it, heated it, battered and broke it to build houses. The houses burned down.

The north circle teases – perhaps a circle, perhaps a concentric circle, perhaps an enormous megalithic horseshoe like others in Brittany, like the trilithons inside Stonehenge – but without lintels. Like the southern ring this also had an internal setting, a gigantic Cove of three gigantic slabs, one fallen and smashed by the same callous, ultimately bankrupted builders.

Outside Avebury were two impressively big and long avenues. The western, leading towards Beckhampton, has gone, its fragments like imprisoned spectres cemented into the walls of houses at Avebury and Avebury Trusloe. Two survive in a field near the Beckhampton traffic island. The Longstones stand close together, Eve the one remaining stone of the avenue, Adam, her ponderous companion, the only sarsen left of a second Cove.

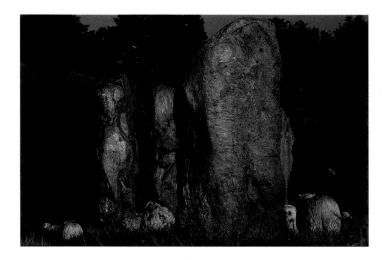

The other avenue, from Avebury's SSE entrance, is better, its stones buried by superstitious mediaeval Christians. To them the Devil was everywhere in this pagan place. The Cove inside the enclosure was the Devil's Brand-Irons. The Cove outside it was the Devil's Quoits. The colossal sarsen by the southern entrance was the Devil's Chair. The chambered tomb towards Marlborough was the Devil's Den. Predictably Avebury's church was built well outside the satanic earthwork.

Less concerned with Lucifer, the employees of the Morven Institute of Archaeological Research, a body formed by Alexander Keiller, member of the Dundee marmalade family, located and re-erected stones in the 1930s. The first of the avenue is missing, its sarsens probably uprooted and splintered by the heartless jobbing builders, led by Tom Robinson, who caused "the most miserable havock of this famous temple", as William Stukeley wrote, calling him "the Herostratus of Avebury". Herostratus was the mid-fourth century BC vandal who for vainglory burned down the Temple of Artemis at Ephesus. At least Robinson did his destruction for money.

The light of the full moon and dawn mingle blue and yellow over the waking sheep

Circles of Stone

One can still walk along part of this resurrected Kennet avenue, noticing the alternating lozenge and pillar shapes of the stones but not appreciating the subtle straightness of the linked sections and not realising how each of the sectors had precious deposits of worked flints or special pottery, even human bones, to sanctify the new stretch.

Keiller did not buy the field beyond, and stones still lie buried there. Others are dumped behind the hedgerow along the road up Overton Hill towards the erstwhile Sanctuary stone circle, now represented by pallid and stumpy pillars of concrete like a vast bagatelle board.

Avebury is a giant amongst megaliths. Even deprived of two-thirds of its stones, interrupted by houses, shops and a pub, with an idiotically dangerous road twisting like a chicane through it, it retains its splendour at the edge of the high downs where the prehistoric Ridgeway trudges. That ancient track is pimpled along its length by silhouetted Bronze Age round barrows signposted by tall trees planted by romantic book-lovers, who read of Gothic horrors in their own private druidical groves.

Avebury, *Afa's burg*, was magical. The titanic sarsen at the north entrance crossed the road at midnight. A ley-line from Land's End to Bury St Edmund's passed through the ring. The Kennet avenue was the petrified bodies of men and women. The Devil intended to bury Avebury because of its Christian resistance but accidentally dropped his spadeful of earth, which became Silbury Hill. Fairies were seen among the stones on bright moonlit nights. Malicious poltergeists caused chaos inside homes in the village.

Best to visit Avebury in the daytime.

Other places of interest. West Kennet megalithic tomb, SU 104 677, is 1½ miles south. Silbury Hill, SU 100 685, is 1 mile south. The Sanctuary stone circle, SU 118 679, is 1½ miles SE. Windmill Hill causewayed enclosure, SU 087 714, is ¼ miles NW. The Devil's Den megalithic tomb, SU 152 696, is 3 miles east.

17
Balnuaran of Clava
Inverness-shire

NH 757 443

Five miles east of Inverness

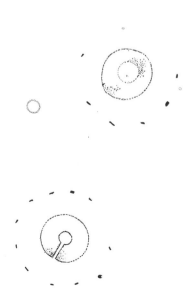

The attractive NE–SW line of the three Clava cairns lies south of Culloden battlefield. The outer cairns are passage-tombs, and between them is a ring-cairn. All stand on artificial platforms. The setting is lovely, with airy trees enclosing the cemetery.

The SW passage-tomb lies inside a 104-foot twelve-stone ring, graded towards the SW. Its ruined tomb, 52 feet across and kerbed, has a south-western entrance. There are cupmarks in the chamber and on a westerly kerbstone. Excavation in 1828 recovered two broken pots and some cremated bone. The central ring-cairn was restored around 1881. It is inside a stone circle 104 feet across. The oval cairn, 60 by 52 feet, has a wide central space. Excavations in 1952 found charcoal and cremated bone there. There are cupmarks on two kerbs. The NE passage-tomb has a graded stone circle 114 by 104 feet across. Excavations in the chamber wrecked in 1854 found "a few bones". Further excavation at Clava in 1996 demonstrated that circle, platform and inner cairn were contemporary structures. To their NW there is a tiny kerb-circle in which masses of white quartz were discovered.

The entrances to the passage-tombs are aligned on the setting midwinter sun which would have shone into their chambers. To the NW, a stone in the SW circle is aligned on the kerb-circles and the rising midwinter sun. There is also a stone in the ring-cairn's circle aligned on the kerb-circle and the rising midsummer sun.

Other places of interest. Culloden battlefield and Visitors' Centre is 1 mile NW. Culdoich ring-cairn, NH 752 438, is 1 mile SSW. Corrimony Clava passage-tomb, NH 383 303, is 25 miles WSW.

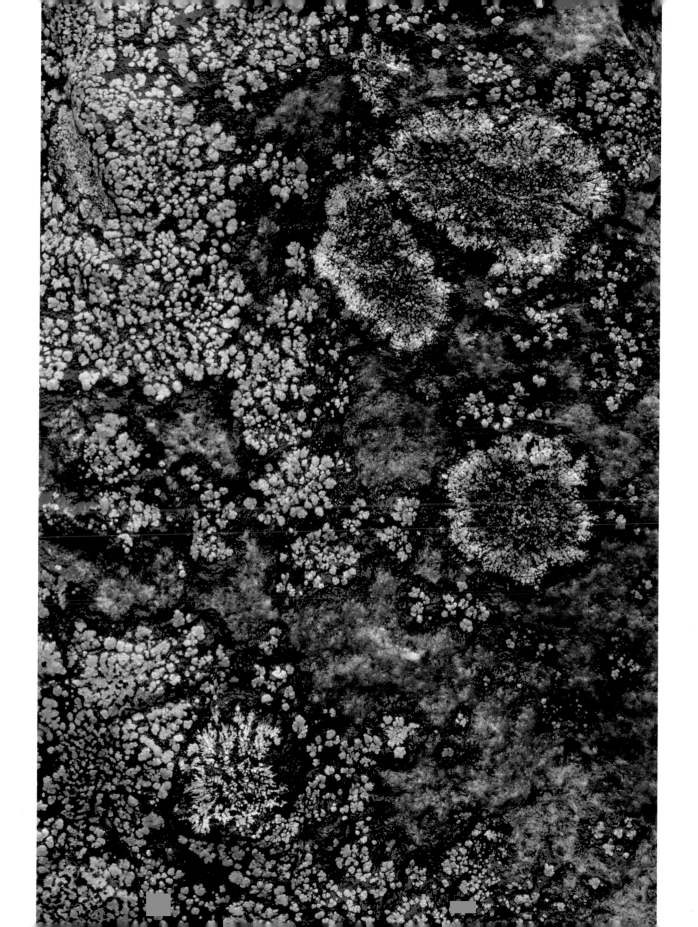

18
Beaghmore
Co. Tyrone

H 685 842

Eight miles WNW of Cookstown

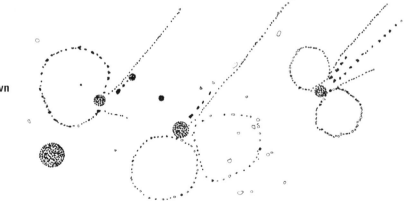

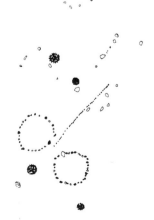

Exposed by peat-cutters, there are three pairs and a single ring in this fascinating complex. Varying from 35 feet to 68 feet in diameter there is not a good circle amongst them. Nine variegated stone rows are attached to the rings and, adding flavour to this Irish archaeological stew, there are a dozen small cairns. Over an area of 1000 square yards Beaghmore was excavated between 1945 and 1949.

At the NE of the group are two very irregular circles with a little cairn between them. Four splayed rows lead to the cairn from the NE, the two outer ones long and of low stones set tangentially to the circles, the inner ones shorter and taller in a typically Irish "high-and-low" arrangement. Beneath them is a collapsed Neolithic field-wall. In the cairn was a cist with a polished porcellanite axe.

To the SW is a second pair of "circles", the northern like a battered rectangle. A "high-and-low" set of rows leads to the central cairn. Under the rings were hearths and Neolithic sherds, the remains of an earlier domestic settlement.

To the NW is an isolated circle whose interior is fearsomely cluttered with a fakir's bed of spiky erect stones and with a tiny cairn embedded in its eastern side. A "high-and-low" pair of rows approaches the cairn from the NE. Under the cairn was a cremation in a cist on top of which were fragments of a human skull.

Well to the SW are two rings side by side and smaller than the others. The northern had a well-defined entrance like others at Broughderg, a mile to the west. A long row of low stones leads to a gap between the circles where a cairn may have been intended.

The majority of the rows were crudely aligned towards the SW and the midwinter sunset. Radiocarbon assays suggest that the Beaghmore rings belong to the centuries between 2000 and 1400 BC.

Other places of interest. The three ruinous Broughderg stone circles, NE, south and SW, H 653 843, are 2 miles west. Davagh Lower ring-cairn and stone row, H 707 867, is 2 miles NE.

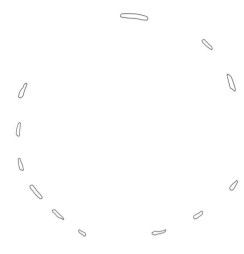

19
Boleycarrigeen
Co. Wicklow

N 938 892

4¼ miles east of Baltinglass

This attractive and unusual embanked stone circle, quite well preserved and enclosed in an earthen ring, has had a variety of local names, a predictable "Druidical circle" and a culinary *Griddle Stones,* reminiscent of Finghal's Cauldron Seat on Arran.

Boleycarrigeen, "the rocky summer pasture", stands high and elusive on the natural terrace of a forested hillside and is often overwhelmed with gorse and bracken. The landscape is spectacular. Brusseltown Ring, 1328 feet O.D., rises 1½ miles to the NNW. It is diminished by the heights of Keandeen Mountain, 2146 feet high, a mile ENE of the stone circle.

Of the original seventeen or eighteen stones of shale, eleven remain, with the stump of a quartz-dense block at ground level. The ring is 45 feet across inside a 6-foot-wide, 3-foot-high bank, its tall, angular slabs contrasting with the rounded granite boulders of another fine Wicklow stone circle, Athgreany, 8½ miles to the north.

Boleycarrigeen's stones are sharply graded to the NE, where the tallest stand over 6 feet high. Oddly, the entrance is opposite, at the SW. The doyen of Irish stone circles, Sean O'Nuallain, observed that "this grading in height is a characteristic of the Cork-Kerry circles and it is quite possible that the builders of the Boleycarrigeen circle were related to those who erected the southern circles".

There appears to be a local, distorted folk-memory of a subterranean Iron Age souterrain in the neighbourhood.

Other places of interest. As well as the circle at Athgreany, N 930 032, there are the remains of a portal-dolmen 5 miles north at Broomsfield near Donard, N 922 983, and a rath at Crossoona, N 932 890, ¾ mile SE.

20
Boscawen-Un
Land's End,
Cornwall

SW 412 274

Four miles SW of Penzance

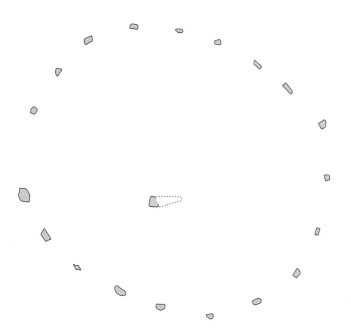

This fine stone "circle", which is actually an ovoid 82 feet by 73 feet, has a tall but markedly leaning stone near its centre. It is believed the pillar was disturbed by treasure-hunters digging at its base. The stones are all of local granite except one of quartz, 4 feet high, at the WSW. "From it the May sun was seen to rise over the centre of the circle", wrote Sir Norman Lockyer in 1909. The ring is composed of nineteen stones, a favoured number for the builders of stone circles on Land's End. There is a wide gap, probably an entrance, at the west.

There are several outlying stones nearby. To the NE at SW 414 276 is the Long Stone, 8 feet 6 inches high, a stout, bent stone just over the brow of the hill. Hedges now hide it from the circle but its top would once have been just visible. Lockyer believed that from the ring it marked the rising of Capella in 2250 BC. There is a fallen stone in the hedge by it. The two may have formed a pair like that at Higher Drift, SW 437 283, between which a grave was discovered.

The stones of the circle puzzle. "Their purpose?" wrote Elizabeth Pepper and John Wilcock, "Nobody knows. But the boy at the farm says visitors come from all over the world to probe and ponder." They would not have enjoyed the muddy, bramble-tangled walk.

Other places of interest. The Merry Maidens stone circle, SW 432 245, is 2¹/₄ miles SE. The Tregeseal ring, SW 387 324, is 3¹/₂ miles NNW. Brane chambered entrance-tomb, SW 401 282, is ³/₄ mile NW. The Neolithic defended settlement of Carn Brea, SW 686 407, is 1¹/₂ miles NW.

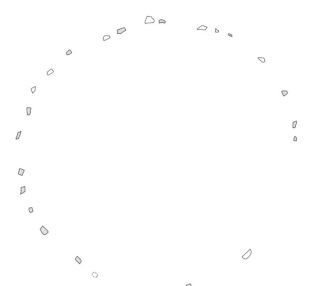

21

Brisworthy
Dartmoor,
Devon

Devon SX 565 655

Three miles ESE of Yelverton

This fine ring stands on a slight, east-facing slope at the edge of Ringmoor Down. Originally there may have been about thirty-six stones, all of local granite, in this ring. Today twenty-four survive, the largest, 3 feet 8 inches high, at the north. The stones are noticeably graded in height, rising to the north and the upward slope. The circle, 81 feet in diameter, was ruinous and was re-erected by human muscle power in 1909 under the supervision of the Rev. H. H. Breton of Sheepstor. The heaviest stone, about 4 tons in weight, required the use of sheer-legs.

During the partial excavation it was discovered that the stones had been held in place by chock-stones in their holes. Traces of charcoal were found in the interior of the ring and this, and the grading, has parallels in the Dartmoor ring of Fernworthy near the Grey Wethers.

Other places of interest. Legis Tor pound settlement, SX 573 654, is 2^1/$_2$ miles east. Ringmoor cairn-circle, SX 563 658, is ^{1}/$_4$ mile NNW.

Circles of Stone

Gneissian granite, one of the oldest rocks in Britain, veined with white quartz

22
Callanish
Isle of Lewis,
Outer Hebrides

NB 213 330

Thirteen miles west of Stornoway

Silhouetted on its ridge against the sea, *Callanish Tursachan*, "the place of sadness", is sometimes known as the Stonehenge of Scotland. It is better than that. With its lovely, lean stones of local gneiss, smooth, swirling with ripples of quartz like fine silk threads, the circle is both an enticement and a challenge. It contains a central pillar that is not central, a tiny chambered tomb inside the ring that is different from every other one on the island, an avenue that sags in the middle, and three short single rows that jut from the ring like spokes of a broken wheel. The ring has been known as *Fir Bhreig*, "the false men", because from a distance the stones resemble a line of human beings.

It is a collection of puzzles containing lines to the sun, moon and stars although it was not an observatory, in a stone circle that was not circular and that began as just one standing stone and ended in destruction, a circle that was derelict by 1000 BC and yet, nine hundred years later, was known to a writer living 1700 miles away. The history is intriguing.

Around 2500 BC, at the beginning of the Bronze Age, on land that had been farmed centuries earlier, a towering stone, 15 feet 9 inches high, and shaped like a ship's rudder, was set up as a landmark for seamen looking for a safe landing-place. Maybe three hundred years later men erected a ring of stones around the weathered column, enshrining it in their new site. The ring was a modestly sized oval, about 44 by 39 feet, of thirteen stones, 10 feet high, visually impressive but capable of holding no more than twenty-five to thirty people in comfort.

Over the decades features were added. Leading to the ring from the sea was a long two-sided avenue like a processional way, closed off at its northern end by a pair of heavy blocks at right angles to the line, and narrowing as its two rows neared the circle. One can imagine men and women moving along the dignified approach. What is not obvious is why prehistoric people also raised three short single rows leading to the ring from the ENE, the south and the west.

They were not pathways. The ENE faced downhill, the southern led to a nearby rocky knoll and the west's end was close to a sudden drop onto a tumble of boulders and outcrops. The plan has been likened to a Celtic cross but if so, one that was markedly buckled, with the ENE arm and NNE avenue deforming its symmetry. The reason for the awkward design appears to be astronomical, and it was Diodorus, a Greek historian of Sicily who died some time after 21 BC, who provided an explanation.

He wrote of a "spherical temple", presumably in Britain. This has been taken to refer to Stonehenge. It does not. The statement that "the moon as viewed from this island appears to be but a little distance from the earth" refers to something impossible at the latitude of Stonehenge, but exactly describes what the southern moon does at Callanish, where it seems to roll along the top of the skyline. The moon, added Diodorus, "dances continually through the night from the vernal equinox and the rising of the Pleiades".

This is remarkable, almost unbelievable, because of three celestial facts about Callanish: the moon, the sun, and the constellation. The avenue is aligned upon the moon's most southerly setting; the western row is aligned upon the equinoctial sunset; and the ENE row is aligned upon the rising of the Pleiades in the years around 1700 BC, a likely time for the building of the short row. The alignments were good but not so precise that they would have been useful to astronomer-priests. They were for nocturnal rituals – but how did Diodorus know?

Change followed. People came to the Outer Hebrides, and inside Callanish, demeaning it, they built a miniature tomb between the central pillar and the eastern stones. Decades later even that burialplace was blocked up. The people went away, and with the increased rainfall of a deteriorating climate peat gradually crept up the stones until a century ago the growth was 6 feet deep. By then there were legends. Giants from the south had put up the great stones. And on Midsummer's Day the "Shining One" walked down the avenue. It is a mystery. Could it be that three thousand years after Callanish had been abandoned there lingered a dim folk-memory of night-time ceremonies as the full moon moved along the outline of the horizon, a time when people celebrated the warmth and richness of the year's summertime?

Other places of interest. Within a few miles of this marvellous site there are other circles: at Ceann Hulavig, NB 230 304, 2 miles SE; Cnoc Ceann a'Gharaidh, NB 222 326, 1/2 mile ESE; Cnoc Fillibhir, NB 225 325, 1/2 mile SE. A well-preserved Iron Age broch can be visited at Dun Carloway, NB 189 412, 4 1/2 miles north.

23
Castle Fraser
Aberdeenshire

NJ 715 125
5¹/₂ miles SW of Kintore

This fine recumbent stone circle stands at the edge of a hill-terrace. The ground on which it is built was levelled by its builders. Sometimes known as *Balgorkar* or as West Mains, it probably once consisted of ten stones and a recumbent. Today six stones stand on the circumference of an impressive circle 67 feet across. Two of the stones are of red granite, four are grey granite, and the recumbent and its flankers are very fine-grained granites veined with white quartz. The stones are noticeably graded in height up towards the recumbent at the SW, which was aligned on the southernmost moonset. Several stones were found to stand in small cairns, as at Loanhead of Daviot.

Inside the ring are the substantial remains of a ring-cairn. Nineteenth-century excavations by Dalrymple discovered an open central space, 13 feet across, lined with slabs. In it were deposits of charcoal and cremated bone. Sherds of a "thick and massive" urn were found by the fallen stone to the west of the west flanker.

In the same field is a pair of standing stones, each about 7 feet in height, one thinly tapering, the other an almost rectangular flat-topped block. They also were in line with the major southern setting of the moon.

Other places of interest. The Lang Stane o'Craigearn, NJ 723 149, is 1¹/₂ miles NE. South Ley Lodge recumbent stone and flankers, NJ 767 132, is 3¹/₄ miles ENE. Sunhoney recumbent stone circle, NJ 716 058, is 4¹/₄ miles south.

Below: The recumbent stone is typical
of north-eastern Scotland

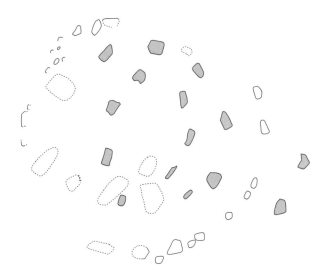

24

Croft Moraig
Perthshire

NN 797 472

Four miles WSW of Aberfeldy

This fine ring, in state care, stands at the NE end of Loch Tay. A concentric ring of local quartzose schist stones stands on a manmade platform, with a pair of standing stones immediately to the east.

Excavation in 1965 revealed a complex history. The first phase, of the Late Neolithic, consisted of about fourteen heavy posts arranged in a horseshoe setting about 26 feet by 23 feet with a natural boulder at its centre. Burnt human bone was found near it. A ditch surrounded the site, and at the east was an "entrance" composed of two short rows of posts.

In a succeeding phase the timbers were replaced by eight stones graded in height towards the SSW, also erected in a horseshoe, 30 feet by 21 feet. A rubble bank was heaped up around it. At the SSW lay a prostrate stone with over twenty cupmarks carved on it. Other cupmarks were ground into the low NE stone.

Finally a circle of twelve stones, about 40 feet in diameter, was erected around the megalithic horseshoe with a pair of stones forming an entrance at the ESE. Graves may have been dug at their bases later.

The platform, the grading, and the supine cupmarked stone at the SW all link Croft Moraig in its later stages with the recumbent stone circles of north-eastern Scotland.

Other places of interest. The Fortingall stone circles, NN 747 470, are 3 1/2 miles west. Cramrar Four-Poster and pair of standing stones, NN 723 452, are 4 3/4 miles WSW.

Middle Period: Early Bronze Age 103

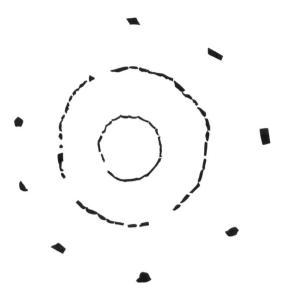

25
Culburnie
Inverness-shire

NH 491 418
3¹/₂ miles SW of Beauly

The location is a chronological muddle. On what had been an open hillside terrace this encircled ring-cairn became overshadowed in a wilderness of trees. Then it was half-walled in the garden of a cottage, whose track from the nearby road tramped through the ring. The prehistoric setting is unrecognisable.

Culburnie, "the small stream with holly bushes", has triumphed over the interference and remains a good example of the Clava monuments around the Moray Firth, a 5-foot-high round cairn, 44 feet across, with an open central space, 17 feet wide. Around the cairn stand eight of the original nine stones of a circle 70 feet in diameter. Folk-memory tells the outcome of the removal of the missing NE pillar by a local mason: "According to popular rumour [he] died a sudden death in consequence of this violation."

Quite predictably the tallest stone of the circle stands at the SSW. The kerb of the cairn inside it has three cupmarks. Like the majority of the Clava cairns the kerb and the circle-stone appear to have been set in line with the most southerly setting of the moon.

Other places of interest. Bruiach ring-cairn, NH 499 414, is ¹/₂ mile SE. Carn Daley Clava passage-tomb, NH 494 314, is 6¹/₂ miles south. Corrimony Clava passage-tomb, NH 383 303, is 10 miles SW.

26

Cullerlie
Aberdeenshire

NJ 785 043
Four miles NW of Peterculter

This ring, now in state care, stands near the roadside on a stretch of low land. The land was once surrounded by swamps, but the circle, 33 feet 5 inches in diameter, was built on a patch of well-drained gravel.

Eight tall stones of coarse red granite were erected here, notably graded in height towards the north. Their bases had been shaped into points to give them more stability in the acidic, treacherous gravel.

When the ring was excavated in 1934 several unusual features were discovered. The site had been levelled and a fire of willow branches had burnt on it, leaving ash lying by the stones. Inside the circle seven small rings of stones, each composed of eleven kerbstones, were constructed around a larger ring, 11 feet across. The excavator commented on the coincidence of eight circle-stones and eight stone rings. Cremated bone and charcoal of oak or hazel were put inside these rings before cairn-stones were heaped above them, covering the deposits.

There was a report of an outlying stone immediately to the west but no trace of it survives.

Other places of interest. Sunhoney recumbent stone circle, NJ 716 058, is 4¹/₂ miles WNW. Midmar Kirk recumbent stone circle, NJ 699 064, is 5¹/₂ miles WNW. The Barmekyn of Echt hillfort, NJ 725 070, is 4 miles NW.

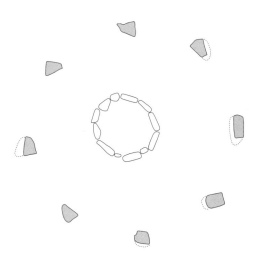

Middle Period: Early Bronze Age   107

A late night flight leaves a light trail down to Aberdeen airport below the ancient ring on Dyce hill

27

Dyce
Aberdeenshire

NJ 860 133

7 ¹/₄ miles SE of Inverurie

This fine recumbent stone circle stands on a shoulder of a hill commanding a superb view to the lowlands and the coast. It is also known as *Tyrebagger*, "the land of acorns".

The ring is still in good condition and consists of ten tall stones and a recumbent on the circumference of a circle 59 feet in diameter. The stones stand in a low stony bank, whitely blotched with lichen. Inside the ring are the remains of a ring-cairn with an outer kerb about 38 feet across.

Because of the awkward shape of the east flanker – a jagged pyramid, against the recumbent – Alexander Keiller, a member of the Dundee marmalade family who was later to excavate at Avebury, concluded in 1934 that the builders had mistakenly interchanged the flanker with the pillar to its east. The west flanker is a tall and shapely pillar. The circle stones are red, gritty granites from a nearby source, but the recumbent, a much broader, squatter stone, is a dark grey granite weighing in the region of 24 tons. It was unstable and now lurches towards the interior of the ring, its broken east shoulder smoothed like solidified tar. The site is spoiled by an electricity pylon that has been erected too close to the circle.

Other places of interest. Broomend of Crichie circle-henge, NJ 779 196, is 6½ miles NW. Castle Fraser (No.23) recumbent stone circle, NJ 715 125, is 9 miles west. There is a nineteenth-century body-snatchers' watch-house in Dyce churchyard.

28

Gors Fawr
Carmarthen,
Dyfed

SN 134 294

3¹/₄ miles ENE of Maenclochog

This ring, "the great heath", stands soggily in the foothills of the Preseli Mountains, from which the bluestones of Stonehenge came. Locally the ring is known as *Cylch y Trallwyn*, "the circle of troubles".

The sixteen much-weathered stones of local doleritic rock noticeably rise in height towards the south, where the tallest is 4 feet 6 inches high. The ring is some 73 feet in diameter. Its grading and size suggest an affinity with the circle at Fernworthy on Dartmoor, a hundred miles SE across the Bristol Channel.

A quarter of a mile to the NNE are two tall outlying stones about 46 feet apart, set at a slight tangent to the ring and arranged NE to SW. Because of the greater height of the horizon to the east the line gives slightly different declinations to the SW and midwinter sunset and the rising midsummer sun to the NE.

Other places of interest. Meini-gwyr circle-henge, SN 142 267, is 1³/₄ miles south. Carn Besi portal-dolmen, SN 149 276, is 2 miles SE. Bedd yr Afanc megalithic tomb, SN 108 345, is 3¹/₂ miles NNW.

29
Grange
Co. Limerick

R 640 410.
Eleven miles SSE of Limerick

Grange circle-henge, sometimes known as the *Lios* or "race-course", is a massive bank of gravelly clay, 30 feet wide, 4 feet high, and 65 yards from crest to crest, with heavy stones standing shoulder to shoulder around the wide interior. There is no ditch.

The stones that fringe its bank are mostly local limestone but some are volcanic breccia from Grange Hill a mile away. Access to the 150-foot-wide interior was provided at the ENE by a narrow stone-lined passage ending inside at two gigantic stones.

In 1939 excavators found a 5-inch-wide posthole at the centre of the ring, too slight for a totem pole but adequate for a post from which the bank could be marked out. Five diameters were fixed, the most important being that from the entrance to an opposing pair of stones, for this was the major axis aligned on the moon's minimum midsummer setting about 2500 BC. Twelve monstrous stones were dragged to the site. Holes were dug two at the entrance, two opposite, where a pair of stones was set up, their tops making a V-notch ideal for sightings. Then, using the stones as markers, the first section of the bank was piled up over the edges of the filled stone holes, flat-topped but with a vertical inner face. A squalid camp for the hundred or more workers sprawled on the west; fires burned, refuse and filth gathered, sporadically strewn over with earth as the months of labour continued. People carried baskets of clay. Others dragged stones. A level clay floor was laid.

The heaviest stone, at the NE, *Rannach Cruim Duibh*, the prominent black stone, weighed over 60 tons, and a hundred men were needed to heave it over a mile and set it up in line with the midsummer sunrise. On 14 May 1785, the effort of building "the large Druidical temple" amazed John Wesley. Comparing Grange with Stanton Drew and Stonehenge, he wrote, "How our ancestors could bring, or even heave these enormous stones what modern can comprehend."

If a date were hazarded for Grange within a century of 2500 BC this would agree with its Neolithic pottery. The presence of food vessels, a bronze awl and coarse pots of the Later Bronze Age are signs of the monument's continuing use well into the second millennium BC.

Other places of interest. Three-quarters of a mile to the ESE, at the south-eastern corner of Lough Gur, is a wedge-tomb, R 646 402. One and a quarter miles to the ENE are ring-forts on Carrig Aille hill. A mile to the NE is an interesting Visitors' Centre.

Car headlights light up the ring and trees

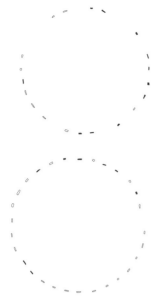

30
Grey Wethers
Dartmoor,
Devon

SX 639 831
2¹/₂ miles north of Postbridge

These paired rings, complete and attractive, are typical of the SW peninsula multiple sites. They stand on open moorland to the west of the Fernworthy reservoir and forest. It is noticeable that they are on either side of a ridge falling gradually and quietly away to north and south. The rings were in collapsed disarray until they were restored in the early twentieth century at the request of King George V. They lie about 20 feet apart, the northern circle having a diameter of 104 feet 6 inches and its partner 108 feet 9 inches. Excavation discovered that the interiors were covered in a spread of charcoal. Pits under two small barrows nearby also contained burnt material.

The granite stones of which the circles are composed probably came from a collapsed tor just to the west. The stones are of fairly even height, 4 to 4¹/₂ feet high. Although entirely natural the jointing of the stones is so regular that they appear to have been dressed and smoothed.

The name *Grey Wethers* is descriptively accurate, because from a distance the stones do resemble quietly grazing sheep. Rumour has it that a stranger was persuaded to buy the flock. It is also said that the stones turn at sunrise and go for a short walk.

Other places of interest. Fernworthy stone circle, SX 655 841, is 1¹/₄ miles NE. Shovel Down stone circle and rows, around SX 660 860, are 2¹/₄ miles NNE. Scorhill stone circle, SX 654 873, is 2³/₄ miles NNE.

Circles of Stone

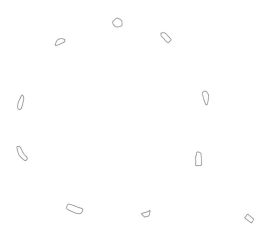

31
Loch Buie
Mull, Outer Hebrides

NM 618 251
A quarter of a mile north of the
ruins of Moy Castle

The graceful ring stands on a rare triangle of fertile land by an isthmus between Loch Buie to the SW and Inch Spelve to the NE. Rhododendron bushes flourish colourfully against it. *Buy,* "yellow", gave the loch its name because of the springtime colour of the hill behind the stone circle.

The large and impressive ring has nine slenderly tall and evenly spaced stones set in a perfect circle 44 feet in diameter. Just to its SE is a low outlier. Two other tall stones stand to the SW. Four hundred yards to the NNW is a large stone standing like a signpost in the direction of Gleinn a Chaiginn Mhoir, the only pass through the mountains to the north.

Three hundred yards to the NW of the circle is a small kerb-circle, much disturbed, with a diameter of about 22 feet. It has a "false" entrance at its SE, a feature of some other small rings in western Scotland such as Temple Wood and Kintraw. The sites stand on ground known as the "Field of the Druids".

Other places of interest. Except for the ruins of the fourteenth-century castle, the first of four successive buildings, there is no archaeological site nearby.

32

Loupin' Stanes
Dumfriesshire

NY 257 966
Eleven miles NE of Lockerbie

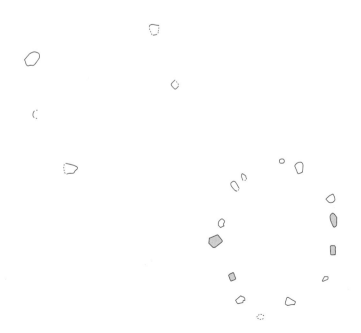

The remains of three rings at the east, SE and NW stand near the east bank of the River White Esk.

The south-eastern ring was erected on an artificial platform that appears to be horizontal. On it twelve stones, ten of them low granite boulders, were raised in a ring about 38 feet in diameter. As at Ninestone Rig in Roxburgh, two much taller stones stand at the SW of the circumference. Such a feature may be related to the recumbent stone circles of north-eastern Scotland. Just to the NW are the almost undistinguishable ruins of a ring perhaps 44 feet across.

About 90 feet to the east of the SE ring are the fallen stones of yet another sub-circular ring that may have a flattened western arc. It measures about 75 feet by 60 feet.

A meandering line of fallen stones that curve around a knoll extend in the direction of the Girdle Stanes stone circle, roughly a third of a mile to the south. That tree-ringed circle-henge is visible from the Loupin' Stanes.

From the south-easterly Loupin' Stanes Alexander Thom calculated that the midsummer sun would set over its ruinous partner to the NW. The line from that wreckage to an outlier on higher ground possibly shows where the sun set at midwinter on a hill behind. Neither Thom nor his son, Archie, could make anything of the scatter of stones to the east of the circles.

Other places of interest. The Girdle Stanes stone circle, NY 254 961, is 700 yards to the SSW. King Schaw's Grave, NY 259 932, is 2 1/4 miles south. Raeburnfoot Roman fort, NY 251 991, is 2 miles north.

Opposite, top: In the foreground the Girdle Stanes circle is cut in two by the White Esk river.
Loupin' Stanes lies half a mile away in the distance

33
Machrie Moor
Isle of Arran

NR 912 324
2¹/₂ miles NNE of Blackwaterfoot

On Machrie Moor, "the fertile plain", six quite dissimilar rings crowd within 350 yards of each other. One was only recently discovered.

Circle XI, the easternmost of the group, was buried under the blanket of peat which now covers the moor and which had submerged the stones. It was excavated by the writer in 1978 and 1979 and by Alison Haggarty between 1985 and 1986, finding that the irregular setting of boulders had replaced a more symmetrical circle of posts.

Two hundred yards to the west, Circle III has one tall pillar of golden sandstone remaining. The stumps of three other slabs still show. The broken tops of these are still there, under the peat. There were nine stones in all, forming an egg-shaped ring like the outer ring of Circle V to the SW. In Circle III there were two cists in the centre, one containing a crouched burial, also some flint flakes.

Circle II, 200 yards to the east, has three tall stones remaining, one a magnificent 17 feet 5 inches high, and two slabs lying inside it, one perforated with the intention of converting it into a millstone. The task was abandoned. Two cists were found inside the ring, one containing a Bronze Age food vessel and four flint flakes from Ireland. A second cist nearby was empty.

Circle I lies just beyond Circle II. It is set out around a precisely drawn ellipse. Granite blocks and sandstone slabs are set alternately round the ellipse, though a slab seems to be missing on the NE. No cist was found in this circle when the writer cleared the overlying turf and peat.

South of Circle III, Site IV now has four lowish granite boulders but it is probably the remains of an Irish Five-Stone ring whose fifth stone was removed when a track was laid out against the circle. It is noticeable that the lowest stone is, as it should be in such a ring, at the SW.

The most westerly of the complex, Circle V, is a concentric known as *Finghal's Cauldron Seat* where the Celtic giant boiled his food. On the SE perimeter of the ring a perforated stone was used by the mythical hero to tether his hound, Bran.

There are also several outlying standing stones. The various graves found demonstrate an Early Bronze Age date for the burials but not for the circles. The cists are almost certainly later additions, as Late

Neolithic assays from Circle I indicate, averaging a period around 2900 BC in the Late Neolithic.

Their site was carefully chosen to be in an isolated area of the moor, standing where a conspicuous notch in the north-eastern hills was in line with the midsummer sunrise.

Other places of interest. Machrie Burn Four-Poster, NR 908 351, is 1³/₄ miles north. Ballymichael Bridge Four-Poster, NR 924 332, is ³/₄ mile east. Auchagallon variant recumbent stone, NR 893 346, is 1³/₄ miles NW. The two Tormore megalithic tombs, NE and SW, NR 903 311, NR 906 324, are 1 mile SW.

Opposite: The sun through autumn clouds

The Merry Maidens stone circle near St Buryan is one of the most perfect in Cornwall. Nineteen stones stand on the perimeter of a perfect circle, 77 feet 9 inches in diameter. A wide gap at the exact east may indicate an original entrance.

The ring is sometimes known as the Dawn's Men, a corruption of *Dans Maen,* "the stone dance", referring to the legend that the stones were girls transmogrified into stone for dancing on the Sabbath.

It is reported that there was once a second circle near the Merry Maidens, at or close to SW 431 244. It seems to have been destroyed in the nineteenth century. Paired rings are not uncommon in Cornwall, examples being known at the Hurlers on Bodmin Moor, at Wendron and at Tregeseal at Land's End.

The chambered tomb of Tregiffian stands by the road downhill. There are several standing stones in the vicinity. Nearly a quarter of a mile to the NW is the pair of stones known as the Pipers. The NE pillar is 15 feet high, the tallest stone in Cornwall. Its partner, 317 feet up the ridge to the SW, is 13 feet 6 inches high. A line extended through their axis would be tangential to the NW stones of the Merry Maidens. Digging near the Pipers in 1871 produced no finds.

Other outlying stones existed 350 yards to the SW of the circle, where there is a pillar 10 feet 6 inches high at SW 427 239. There were once two stones here, at Boscawen Ros, but they were thrown down and only the one was re-erected.

Other places of interest. At SW 429 245, ¼ mile west, is the menhir of *Goon Rith,* "Red Downs", also known as the Fiddler. It is 10 feet 6 inches high. An excavation in 1871 found nothing except a beach pebble. Immediately across the road from the Merry Maidens is a holed stone, SW 432 246, re-used as a gatepost.

34

Merry Maidens
Land's End, Cornwall

SW 433 245
4 miles SW of Penzance

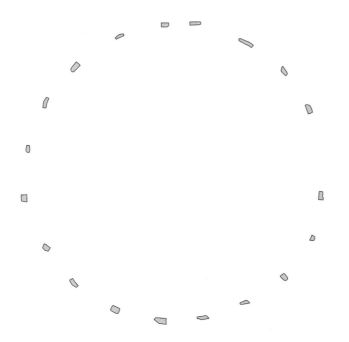

Wearing its vegetation like a fur collar or grass skirt, this rock seems more than ever like a dancing maiden

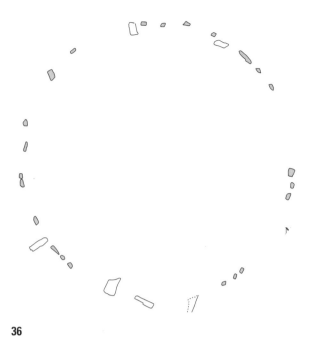

36
Scorhill
Dartmoor,
Devon

SX 654 873

Three miles west of Chagford

This is a confused and battered site. *Scaur Hill* or "the wooded hill" is now a misnomer for there are no trees on the bare hill-slope. Yet the ring could be one of the finest in the SW of England were it not for the two ghastly tracks that plough their way through it. Fewer than the original seventy or so jaggedly pointed stones survive in what was a true circle about 88 feet across, large for Dartmoor and one of several big stone circles in the north-eastern corner of the moor presumably for large groups of people settling and farming in this hospitable part of Dartmoor. Several stones were taken to repair a tin-miners' leat about fifty yards to the west.

The tallest pillar, at the NW, has apparent cupmarks on its inner face but they are geological accidents. However, like the "cupmarked" slab at Cong in Ireland, this stone may have been chosen for its magical appearance.

The circle has an unpleasant reputation. Horsemen have said that they cannot take their mounts through it because something disturbs them and it is often necessary to ride around the ring rather than pass through it. An authority on the folk stories of Dartmoor, Ruth St Leger-Gordon, wrote, "It is, of course, notorious that horses are extraordinarily sensitive to, and terrified of, the smell of blood … The stone circles were in all probability scenes of rough justice, perhaps even of sacrifice and ritual murder." It is recorded that faithless wives were compelled to wash in Cranmere Pool, then run round the Scorhill circle three times before going to the River Teign where they had to pass through a large holed stone in the water. From there they had to travel, drenched, exhausted and, doubtless, regretful, to the pair of the Grey Wethers stone circles three hilly miles to the south, where they prayed for forgiveness – if they still had any interest in life.

Other places of interest. Kestor Bronze Age settlement, SX 665 867, is ³/₄ mile to the SE. Shovel Down stone circle and rows, SX 660 860 is 1 mile south. The paired Grey Wethers stone circles, SX 638 832, are 2³/₄ miles SSW.

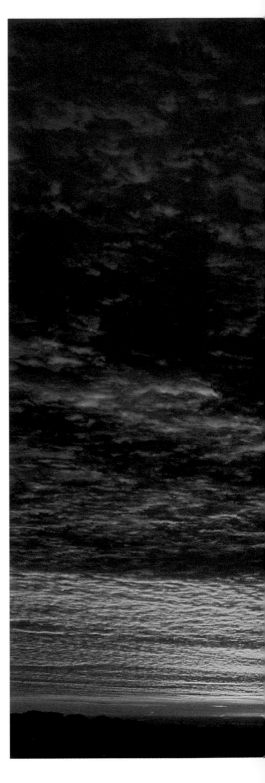

Dawn on winter solstice

37

Stonehenge
Wiltshire

SU 122 422

7 1/2 miles north of Salisbury

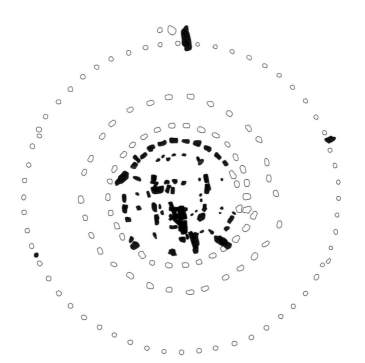

For centuries Stonehenge was the stage for grim ceremonies of death and darkness. The circle began with night, had a sunlit interlude and then returned to night before being deserted in the cold emptiness of Salisbury Plain. "Did they sacrifice to God here?" asked Tess. "No," said Angel, "I believe to the sun." Thomas Hardy was right.

Five thousand years ago men dug out the circular ditch of a ring a hundred yards across and heaped its chalk onto an inner bank. They left a narrow gap at the south and a wider one at the NE. Outside it stood a heavy and coarse pillar, a sarsen from the sandstone slopes of the Marlborough Downs to the north. The stone's position had been carefully calculated.

The new earthwork was a simple enclosure, a henge, but at its centre, invisible today, there was an enormous timber structure. Bones of oxen, human jaws and bones there hint that it was a mortuary house to which corpses had been carried until their dried, broken skeletons could be taken away for burial. From its beginning Stonehenge stood at the heart of a six-mile-wide cemetery. Long barrows lay all around it, mounds with wooden chambers in which the dead were interred.

Stonehenge from the sky on summer solstice morning

The barrows faced anywhere from NE to SE in an arc between the midsummer and midwinter risings of the moon, and at Stonehenge the NE entrance also looked towards the horizon where the midwinter moon rose at the northernmost of its 18¹/₂-year cycle. The outlying pillar, the Heel Stone, stood exactly halfway along that cycle, warning onlookers that when the moon appeared to its left it would reach its northernmost rising four years later. To the people the moon may have been the home of the dead.

Death was Stonehenge's constant companion. Just inside the circumference of the bank fifty-six ragged holes were dug, now named after their discoverer, the seventeenth-century antiquarian John Aubrey. In them were washed, burnt bones of human beings. In the ends of the ditch against the two entrances were other cremations, probably of a mother and child, sacrifices to give power to the henge. The bones of another child had been buried at the SE in line with the rising of the midsummer moon. Everything was nocturnal.

Years later there was change. The people went away. Weeds and bushes spread in a wilderness across the earthwork. The building decayed. Then Stonehenge was reborn. People of a different cult came. They widened the NE entrance thus changing the axis, creating the illusion that the Heel Stone stood almost in line with the midsummer sunrise. From being a lunar sanctuary Stonehenge was transformed into a solar temple.

An earth-banked avenue was laid out towards the entrance, and along it were dragged scores of bluestones glaciated from SW Wales a hundred and fifty miles to the west. The man-sized blocks formed a concentric circle at the centre of the earthwork where the building had been. Around the two rings, at the corners of a spacious rectangle whose short sides pointed to the midsummer sunrise and the long sides to the northern setting of the moon, stood the Four Stations, unshaped sarsens, from whose ESE stone an observer would have seen the May Day sun set behind the WNW Station.

The rings were never finished. They were removed and replaced by a more ambitious project. Around 2600 BC, near the beginning of the Early Bronze Age, dozens of gigantic sarsens, up to 30 feet long and 50 tons in weight, were brought from the Marlborough Downs about twenty miles away. It was an awesome undertaking.

Stonehenge never conformed to the pattern of traditional stone circles. The hard sandstones were battered and ground into smoothness, were shaped into mortice-and-tenon joints, tongued-and-grooved,

Druids chant incantations on winter solstice eve (opposite)

chamfered. It was carpentry by native woodworkers of Salisbury Plain as though translating the ancient wooden building into everlasting stone. The ring was 97 feet across and lintelled like the ring-beams of a house.

Inside its perfect circle five tall archways of lintelled trilithons, "three stones", were set up in a huge horseshoe open to the NE. They steadily rose in height to the climax of the 24-foot-high Great Trilithon at the SW. Change continued. The bluestones were brought back. The majority were placed in an untidy ring inside the sarsen circle; nineteen others were meticulously shaped into elegant 6–9-foot-high pillars arranged in a U-shaped setting inside the trilithon horseshoe. A 10-foot-high pillar of

Welsh sandstone, the Altar Stone, stood near the centre. At the NE entrance two stones, the so-called Slaughter Stone and another, stood side by side. A comparable partner was given to the Heel Stone. Through the narrow gap between the four pillars the midsummer sunrise shone into the circle and onto the Altar Stone.

Death remained. The interior of Stonehenge was confined, closed in by the rings of stone, the trilithons and the Altar Stone, and only a few chosen people could stand there. It was a secret place. Stone stood in front of stone. Commoners outside the earthwork could see nothing of the rites inside. They knew only that this was the dead time of the year

and that there were arcane symbols of death on the stones.

As the élite moved from the avenue and into the circle they saw carvings of axes on the outer surfaces of stones at the east. Inside the ring the group passed between a low, flat-topped block and a pointed stone, images of male and female fertility. The Altar Stone rose before them like an embodiment of a female guardian of the dead. To its left, on the inner face of a trilithon, were carvings of a bronze dagger and axes, the weapons of the protectress so often to be found on tombs in Brittany, a few miles across the English Channel. To the right, opposite, on another trilithon, was a rectangular carving, another image of her. Above it was another carving of an axe. It was sacred space. Everything was redolent of death and the rebirth of life. Above the Altar Stone, between its top and the lintel of the Great Trilithon, the midwinter sun sank into the darkest, shortest time of the year.

Nothing endured. Once more Stonehenge was abandoned. Stones fell in the snow and hail and rain of the Iron Age. Roman tourists who visited the ruin lost coins and trinkets in the long grass growing over the remains of the unsuspected dead.

Other places of interest. The intriguing site of Woodhenge, SU 150 434, is a mile NE. The Winterbourne Stoke long- and round-barrow cemetery, SU 101 417, is is 1 1/2 miles WSW. The Wilsford barrow cemetery, SU 118 398, is 3/4 mile SSW. The Iron Age hillfort and Norman motte of Old Sarum, SU 137 327, is 6 miles south, near Salisbury.

38
Temple Wood
Argyllshire

NR 827 979

Six miles NNW of Lochgilphead

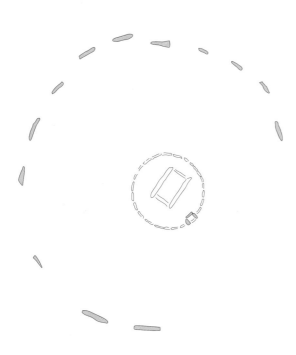

In the megalithic paradise of the Kilmartin Valley Temple Wood is the only stone circle. Sometimes known as Half Moon Wood, it stands against a line of impressive cairns, one of them, Nether Largie South, a chambered tomb, another, Nether Largie North, with an internal cist-slab covered in carvings of bronze axes. Nearby are the lunar Kilmartin Stones.

Excavations in 1928–9 and between 1974 and 1980 discovered the site of a small northern ring, first an enigmatic timber setting of the early fourth millennium BC that was later transformed into an unfinished stone circle.

Just to its south was the better-known stone "circle", in fact an ellipse 44 feet 7 inches north–south by 39 feet 8 inches. It began as an open ring. The northern stone had carvings of two large spirals, the eastern anti-clockwise, the western clockwise. A stone at the NNE had a rough motif of concentric circles. Suggestively, the stone at the north and one opposite at the south were chlorite schists, a different mineral from other slabs in the ring. This emphasis on a north–south alignment was common to both rings.

The ring was converted into a ring-cairn by the addition of drystone walling between the stones. At the centre a large cist contained a cremation. It was not the end of alteration. The drystone walling was thrown down and slabs on edge were set edge-wise between the stones and across the entrance. Kerb-cairns were added inside the circle, the whole setting surrounded by a heavy, wide bank. It is pleasing to see that after all this disturbance the site has been very charmingly restored.

Other places of interest. Nether Largie North round cairn, NR 831 985, is ½ mile NE. Nether Largie South chambered tomb, NR 828 979, is ¼ mile east. The Ballymeanoch standing stones, NR 834 964, are 1 mile SSE. Ri Cruin decorated cist, NR 825 972, is ½ mile SW.

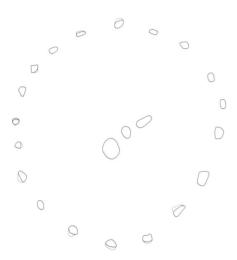

39

Torhousekie
Wigtownshire

NX 383 565

3 1/4 miles **WNW of Wigtown**

This splendid ring stands at the edge of a low terrace on the Machars, a stretch of sandy, fertile land. Nineteen stones, rising in height towards the SE, stand on the circumference of a ring 69 feet in diameter. They are all of local granite. At the centre of the circle are three rounded boulders, the two larger flanking a smaller slab in an arrangement reminiscent of a recumbent and its flankers but unusually facing SE. Extending to the NW behind the setting is a D-shaped rubble bank like a form of ring-cairn.

In 1889 a cairn near Torhousekie had a cist-slab taken from it for a drain-cover. "Six different persons said that they repeatedly saw, after nightfall, a light move from the cairn, follow the track by which the stone was carried, and settle on the top of it for a short time. These people are afraid to open any more cairns!"

Other places of interest. Just over 100 yards to the east, alongside the lane at the head of a slight rise, is a short row of three boulders rising in height towards the SW, aligned on the midwinter sunset. A reported stone circle at NX 382 566 no longer exists. Cairns and standing stones are NX 352 581, 2¼ miles NW. Boreland Clyde-Solway chambered tomb, NX 405 690, is 8 miles NNE.

40
Ardblair
Perthshire

NO 160 439
1¹/₂ miles WSW of Blairgowrie

This disturbed ring, sometimes known as the Leys of Marlee, is divided by the B 947 road. It is typical of the Six-Stone rings in this part of Scotland, its stones now standing on the circumference of a ring, 49 feet across, already ruinous when the road was laid about 1856; two of the stones were re-erected at that time. The NW stone is well out of position today but the stones appear to be graded in the customary manner of NE and central Scotland.

Alexander Thom was puzzled by the irregular shape of the ring but deduced that "a road runs through the ring and some of the stones may have been moved to clear the ditch". The road is straight. The traffic is fast.

Other places of interest. The paired Broad Moss stone circles, NO 198 488, are 3³/₄ miles NNE. At Meigle, NO 287 445, 8 miles east there is a fine collection of carved Pictish slabs. There are hut-circles, NO 116 482, 3¹/₂ miles NW.

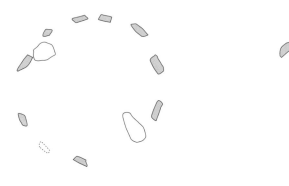

41
Ardgroom
South-West
Co. Cork

V 707 553

Five miles SW of Lauragh

Miles to the west of Cork, "the two ridges", also known as Canfea, overlooks the wide River Kenmare. Far from the road, wrongly signposted and half-wrecked, this circle remains spectacular, its tall brown pillars, streaked with white, pointing like chilled fingers from the tussocks of boggy grass. It is not a typical recumbent stone circle, for the recumbent itself, far from lying prostrate, actually stands a thin pillar, 4 feet high, mingling comfortably with its partners. Twenty feet to its east an 8-foot-high outlying stone is angled towards the ring.

Other places of interest. Half a mile ENE, at V 738 563, are the remains of the most elusive recumbent stone circle in Ireland, Ardgroom North-East. Cashelkeelty Five-Stone ring, V 748 573, 3 miles NE. Shronebirrane recumbent stone circle, V 753 554, is 3 miles east.

42
Backhill of Drachlaw
Aberdeenshire

NJ 673 464
Four miles SW of Turriff

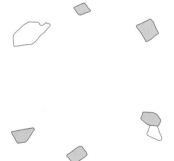

This ring on the south-eastern slopes of Drach Law, "the hill of drakes", was once an elegant ring of six stones. It is interesting for three reasons. Once it was a tiny oval of six large boulders, a contrast between smallness and size of stones like that at South Ythsie, near Ellon, 17 miles to the SE. Both unusual rings were set up on the outskirts of the heartland of recumbent stone circles, from which their architecture is descended.

The dark quartz-pitted boulders of Backhill of Drachlaw were set in a ring 28 by 24 feet on a long NE by SW axis. There is an architectural oddity. The three blocks on the west lie as usual along the circumference of the ring, but those on the east stand radially across the perimeter.

The long axis is emphasised by the fact that the lowest at the NE lies opposite the tallest at the SW, a boulder that had fallen and was re-erected in 1903 – but badly: it has fallen again. It may have been aligned on the midwinter sunset.

There had been an almost identical ring just to the west with six stones in a ring some 28 feet across. In the nineteenth century a tenant wanted "a block of good stone out of which to make lintels" and chose the largest and shapeliest. Later, the remainder were taken to be broken and used for field-walls.

Other places of interest. Two hundred yards to the NE, at NJ 674 465, is the queerest of all recumbent stone circles, at Cairn Riv: the recumbent itself is not a long prostrate block but a tall and grotesquely thick pillar.

43
Balmuick
Perthshire

NN 785 247
Two miles NNE of Comrie

On a high hill five miles from Crieff there are six stones, five of them fallen, one standing about 5 feet tall. These may be the remains of a typical Perthshire Six-Stone ring. They may equally be the remains of a typical Perthshire Four-Poster which had an outlying pair of stones to its east. It was thought that one of the prostrate slabs had been the capstone of a central cist, and it is noticeable that the interior of the site is smoothly and neatly dished, running around the circumference of a circle some 13 feet across, rather like the kerbs of a ring-cairn. A much smaller, sub-rectangular slab has a crudely cut circular hole at its centre, the abandoned attempt to convert it into a millstone.

Other places of interest. There are long views from the elevated site. A nineteenth-century antiquarian wrote, "Looking south-westwards we can descry . . . three great cairns", from one of which came an unusual handled food vessel.

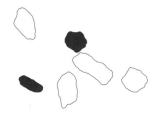

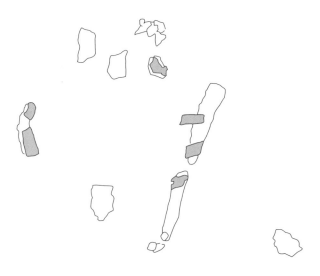

44
Bohonagh
Co. Cork

W 308 368

1½ miles east of Ross Carbery

A mile from the sea, at the head of a hillside and overlooking a neat chessboard of fields like rumpled tartan, *Bohonagh*, "the place of cattle" or "the yellow stream", is one of the most monumental of the large recumbent stone circles in the county. It has not been dated but is almost certainly a contemporary of Drombeg only three miles to its west. The diameters are comparable, here about 32 feet.

In both rings a central cremated pit-burial was found. At Bohonagh the excavation of 1959 discovered that the area had been stripped of turf before a shallow rock-cut pit was dug, cremated bone deposited and a low mound of earth piled over it.

The thirteen grey stones are blotched with quartz, and sizeable blocks of quartz were used as packing to support the standing stones. The recumbent, a big, squat boulder, lies ponderously at the west. Opposite, the portal stones are 8 feet high and arranged radially to form a dominating entrance. The east -west axis of the ring points very approximately to sunset at midyear.

Twenty-seven feet south of the circle the excavator found the post-holes of a spacious, rectangular hut. Only a few flint flakes were recovered but the proximity of the hut to the ring makes it likely that the two were associated.

A heavy boulder-burial can be seen just to the east. Its capstone, about 8 feet square, a foot thick and weighing a back-straining 4 tons, has seven weathered cupmarks on it. Cremated bones were found but no grave-goods.

Other places of interest. There are recumbent stone circles at Drombeg, W 247 352, 4 miles WSW; at Reanascreena, W 265 410, 3 miles NW; and at Knocks, W 299 457, 6 miles north.

45

Bryn Cader Faner
Merioneth,
Gwynedd

SH 648 353

Five miles NE of Harlech

This, "the great stronghold on the hill", is one of the most dramatic of all stone circles. It is also a possible hybrid, a plain, open circle of about thirty stones that was later half-submerged in an untidy round cairn whose little kerbstones are barely detectable.

The top of the cairn was dug into before the First World War, leaving an untidy pit, about 8 by 4 feet, at the bottom of which lie three toppled slabs from a pillaged cist. It is doubtful whether the labourers were satisfied.

The stone circle was untouched until the Second World War, when licentious soldiery pulled out half the stones and broke others. Despite this vandalism the monument remains spectacular. On a rocky knoll to the west of Moel Ysgyfarnogod, fifteen stones lean out from the cairn like dragon's teeth, perhaps pushed outwards by the weight of the cairn-stones around them. From the north nothing can be seen until one is almost against the site, but from the south it occupies a false crest and is outlined sharply against the sky.

"It was sited in this way", wrote Bowen and Gresham, "so that it might be seen on the skyline by those who approached it along the trackway from the south . . . It is possible to assume from this fact that the dead person for whom the cairn was built lived somewhere in the direction of the south, and that the body was carried from there up the trackway to its last resting-place, visible all the way on the skyline, near the highest point to which the route climbs."

Other places of interest. There are the remains of cairn-circles ¹/₂ mile north at SH 640 359. There is a Roman altar at Tan yr Allt, 5¹/₂ miles NW, at SH 574 403. Harlech castle is 5 miles SW.

46
Carrigagulla
Co. Cork

W 370 834
Seven miles NNE of Macroom

Of all the delicately elegant rings in SW Ireland, Carrigagulla, "the rocky hill-shoulder", must be a leading contender. "This circle is the largest and best-preserved that I have yet seen", wrote that megalithic ring enthusiast, John Condon, in 1917 and his words remain true today. In a pleasant field, a plantation behind it, the recumbent stone circle is in an almost immaculate state of preservation, and thirteen of a probable fifteen stones survive, thin slabs of sandstone like a child's playthings.

A well-set block, once upright, lies near the centre of the ring. But in one respect Condon was inexperienced. Further fieldwork would show him that Carrigagulla's diameter of some 30 feet was common among the recumbent stone circles of Co. Cork, and it has been suggested that it was obtained through the use of a unit of measurement of about 3 feet.

The ring's two entrance stones stand at right angles to the circumference like portals, and opposite them the recumbent is a model of perfection, only 1 foot 4 inches high but a full 5 feet 6 inches in length. The proportions are beautiful. And with an ENE–WSW axis of about 245° the circle seems to have been aligned on the midwinter sunset.

Other places of interest. There is a good Five-Stone ring in the next field, 415 yards NE, W 371 838, but now probably trapped and hidden in a growing plantation. There is a Three-Stone row, W 371 829, 1/2 mile south, and another, W 383 829, 3/4 mile east.

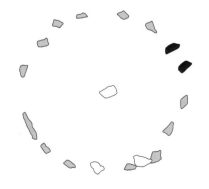

48

Cong
Co. Mayo

M 163 558
Three-quarters of a mile NE
of Cong

So damaged are three of the four sites that it is not surprising that Estyn Evans thought them "best interpreted as the kerbs of round cairns which have been removed". They are not. There are indeed several vast cairns in the mystical neighbourhood, with its subterranean streams and stalactites, but not at Cong.

Those sites are stone circles and it is the northernmost that is the marvel, a variant multiple circle whose uninformed builders not only misplaced the recumbent stone and its flankers but seem also to have overlooked some architectural elements altogether.

This is a well-proportioned circle, about 54 feet across, erected on a platform cut into the natural slope. Inside the ring is a kerbed cairn. Eighteen of probably an original thirty stones still exist. At the north is the Co. Mayo version of a recumbent stone, a neatly rectangular block, some 4 feet long and 3 feet high, with flankers on either side of it.

Across the ring at the SW one of the two portals has gone, but its south-eastern partner must have seemed, to the wondering people who found it and rejoicingly brought it here, to be imbued with a weird power, for its inner face is pockmarked with a honeycomb of deep depressions like the handiwork of a fanatic obsessed with cupmarks. The stone circle is a megalithic marvel, far from its forgotten ancestry in SW Ireland, airily enshrined in tall, lean trees, enduring in a region where megalithic rings are scarce.

Other places of interest. There are great cairns in the vicinity. Ballymacgibbon round cairn, covering a passage-tomb, M 183 555, is 1 mile east. Eochy's Cairn, perhaps with an internal chambered tomb, M 170 630, is 4½ miles north. It is opposite the overgrown fort of *Cathair Phaiter*, "the Pewter Fort".

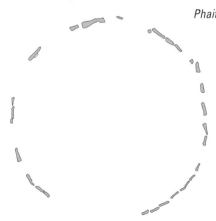

Down Tor – which should be called after Hingston Tor, on which it stands – is a fine example of the parochial Dartmoor megalithic hybrid, an impressive 36-foot circle of substantial stones surrounding the tumbled humps of a cairn with an even more disturbed cist at its heart, and connected to a long single row of 160 stones that trudge south-westwards uphill for 382 yards to the ring. They steadily rise in height, from a 5-foot-high terminal stone which is a dwarf when contrasted with the monstrous 9-foot-6-inch-high angular pillar against the stone circle. Having fallen, it was set up again in 1884, concreted in a pit deeper than the original stonehole.

Behind the circle the higher slopes of the tor are littered with its collapse of boulders, whose abundance made the task of the circle-builders less arduous.

The Rev. Hugh Breton remembered that "the stones were tampered with in 1880, but the Rev. S. Baring-Gould and Mr Robert Burnard came to the rescue, and saved this beautiful monument from destruction, in the same way as they have saved so many. They repaired the damage done, and re-erected fallen stones."

Looking down the row from the circle there is a second overgrown cairn on the nearer slope. To its left are the grassy banks of a pound where cattle were confined. Inside the enclosure are two hut-circles, and it is tempting to see in this settlement, so close to the row and stone circle, the homes of the people who used the ring. There is nothing to prove or disprove the thought.

49
Down Tor
Dartmoor,
Devon

SX 587 694
Four miles ENE of Yelverton

Other places of interest. An area exploited by tin-miners can be made out at SX 582 697. The Drizzlecombe rows are 1¹/₂ miles SSE at SX 592 671. Yellowmead (No.70) multiple circle, SX 575 678, is ¹/₄ mile SSW.

Wild Dartmoor ponies graze along the avenue stones

Other places of interest. Fifty yards to the west are circular huts and another "stone circle" which in fact was a *fulacht fiadh*, an Irish term for a cooking-place. Piles of burnt stones, pot-boilers, were heaped around it. It was of the early Christian period.

The Plough sits in the autumn sky beneath the light of the full moon. Above, moonlight shadows.

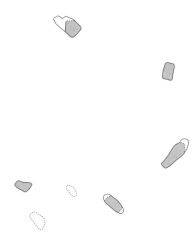

51
Duddo Four Stones
Northumberland

NT 931 437
Seven miles SW of Berwick

The situation is superb. The tall, shapely pillars stand like a pollarded spinney, sharp against the skyline, on the top of a flat knoll 40 feet above the surrounding countryside. The position is splendid. The arithmetic is not.

Known as Duddo Four Stones since the eighteenth century, there are actually five of an original eight. From 5 feet to 7 feet 6 inches high, the coarse local sandstones are grooved and runnelled from centuries of rain on their exposed ground. It is clear that the ring, about 32 feet across, has been disturbed and reconstructed, for the stones at the north and SE stand askew to the circumference. The latter was re-erected in 1903. Some twenty years earlier Mr Robert Carr had dug inside the circle, discovering two stoneholes at the NW and noticing an irregular depression at the centre containing "much charcoal and bone". There are six or seven cupmarks on the inner face of the SW stone, perhaps placed in line with the midwinter sunset.

The stones of *Duddo*, "the mound and valley of Dudda", perplexed villagers. Some believed the ring to be a memorial to Scots killed at the forgotten skirmish of Grindon Marsh in 1558. Others more imaginatively saw the circle as the bodies of men turned to stone for digging up turnips on the Sabbath. In reality it is a shrine, sanctified with human bone, for the rituals of a Bronze Age family.

Other places of interest. It is an isolated site. Hethpool stone circles, NT 892 278, are 10 miles SW. Ilderton circle, NT 971 205, is 14 miles to the SSE.

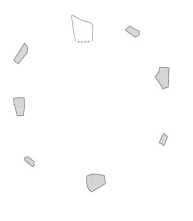

52
Duloe
Cornwall

SX 235 583

Four miles SSW of Liskeard

Called *Duloe* because it stands between the two rivers of the East and West Looe this lovely stone circle is distinctive for three reasons. It is very small, an oval of no more than 39 feet north–south by 35 feet. Despite this its eight stones are remarkably tall; the biggest, 8 feet 6 inches high, is at the south, at the end of the long axis. Duloe's third distinction is that although it was constructed on an extensive area of Old Red Sandstone its pillars are all vividly white, glittering quartz, a unity virtually unique amongst stone circles. There is a broad deep seam of quartz at Dupath Well, 11 miles to the NE, but this is too far away to be the source of the Duloe pillars.

There appears to have been an indifferent attempt to alternate the size of the stones, larger against smaller, rather like the "male" and "female" pillars and blocks known elsewhere, but the result is not convincing.

When a hedge was being removed in the middle of the nineteenth century the circle was damaged and the northern stone broken. Charcoal was unearthed. The labourers also contrived to smash a fine Cornish ribbon-handled urn of the Bronze Age.

Being in an area of extensive cultivation no worthwhile megalithic monuments have been preserved in the vicinity of the ring.

Other places of interest. Castle Dore, an "Arthurian" earthwork, SX 103 548, is 8¹/₂ miles WSW. Hall Wood circular encampment, SX 215 555, is 2¹/₄ miles SW.

53
Glantane
Co. Cork

W 280 833
4¹/₂ miles south of Millstreet

Here is a romantically reticent ring, set in a little grove, walled in behind an abandoned farmhouse. Everything here is green, the leaves of the trees, the thickly luscious grass, the stones green with the moss of ages. In this quiet setting everything seems half as old as time, as silent as a forgotten crypt. The atmosphere encloses one as Andrew Marvell sensed,

> Annihilating all that's made
> To a green thought in a green shade.

At *Glantane*, "the little glen", the stones were once new, clean, set in a modest circle no more than 16 feet across, the biggest of the boulders only 3 feet high, its companions declining from the portal to the lowest of all, the recumbent near the south of the ring. Its azimuth of 192° has no association with either the sun or the moon.

Other places of interest. There are other stone circles nearby: Knocknakilla, W 297 841, is 2 miles NNE; Carriganimmy, W 293 827, is ³/₄ mile SE; Cabragh, W 278 798, is 2¹/₂ miles south.

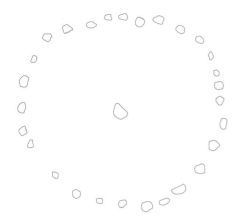

Standing on Cambret Moor, whose name is often given to the site, the otherwise unremarkable ring of *Glenquickan*, "the valley of Kirkmabreck", has the finest of all central pillars, a sturdy giant's thumb of grey granite over 6 feet high, 3 feet wide and over 2 feet thick. Probably about 8 feet long, it must weigh over 4 tons, and at least twenty men would have been needed to haul it upright. It is one of the most impressive stones in this lonely part of SW Scotland.

Around it is a ring of about thirty low boulders forming an oval 53 by 49 feet, the short axis lying almost exactly north–south. Inside is a spread of cobbling, hinting that the origins of such stone circles lay in the kerbed cairn tradition, and it is very likely that the "stone circle" was constructed around a long-standing pillar that may originally have been a trackway marker across the empty wastes of the moor.

Other places of interest. Claughreid circle, NX 517 560, is 1¹/₂ miles SE. Cauldside Burn circle and cairn, NX 529 571, is 1¹/₂ miles SE. The two Cairnholy chambered tombs, NX 517 538, are 2¹/₂ miles SE.

54

Glenquickan
Kirkcudbrightshire

NX 509 582
Six miles WNW of Gatehouse of Fleet

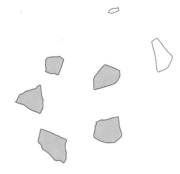

Sometimes known as *auchlaicha*, "the field of stones", the ring is exposed on a "lonely and elevated spot" at a height of 1240 feet O.D. From the site there are magnificent views of mountains, cultivated countryside and the lovely waters of Loch Tay. Two fast-flowing burns run to east and west of the circle.

Only four of the original nine stones still stand, with two more prostrate, separated by the wall of the 1850s whose builders had robbed the ring for material.

In 1942 the ring suffered a disorganised excavation. At the centre was "a dark deposit. It extended over a space of 2 feet square, and was about 5 inches in depth. It was mixed with a white limy substance consisting of calcined bones . . . The surrounding soil is a reddish colour"; this was the surviving evidence of the pyre that had burnt the dead body before the final burial.

Other places of interest. The Fortingall stone circles, NN 747 470, are 2¹/₂ miles NW. Croft Moraig stone circle, NN 797 742, is 3¹/₂ miles NE. Cramrar Four-Poster and pair of standing stones, NN 723 452, are 3 miles NW.

55

Greenland
Perthshire

NN 767 427

6¹/₄ miles SE of Aberfeldy

In the garden of the Old Toll House is the "Remains of Druids" Temple (supposed). At the end of the nineteenth century the site was threatened by the laying of a pipeline from the Talla Water, but the ring was saved. According to an earlier report it stood "in a hamlet called Harestanes, which derived its name from certain Standing Stones of unknown antiquity".

The ring did not belong to the natural animal family Leporidae. Its associations were more sinister. It had also been known as the "Witch's Stones" because the hare or *haer*, like black cats and bats, was thought to be a familiar of witches, and the circle, despite its cramped interior, was believed to be the haunt of covens. In the twelfth century Gerald of Wales wrote of witches who "changed themselves into the shape of hares that, sucking teats under this counterfeit form, they might stealthily rob other people's milk".

Perhaps to diminish its evil, the Harestanes ring has been abused. Today there are only five massive, pale-red rough blocks crudely forming a ring of which the north-eastern arc is missing. The circle was once about 10 feet across. A slight slab, now fallen, once stood outside.

In Scotland there has been a minor cult of enclosing circles in gardens. At Auchlee in Aberdeenshire the astonishment of a recumbent stone circle was recently found in one. Another was domesticated at Culburnie (No.25) in Inverness-shire. At *Tigh-na-Ruaich*, "the house in the heather", near Pitlochry, a ring of six tall pillars was discovered when a wilderness of brambles and gorse was removed in 1855.

Other places of interest. The ruined but archaeologically interesting cairns of Drumelzier, NT 123 326, and Woodend, NT 121 313, are 4 and 6 miles SW.

56

Harestanes
Peeblesshire

NT 124 43
7¹/₂ miles WNW of Peebles

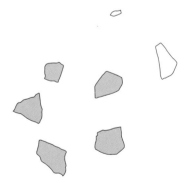

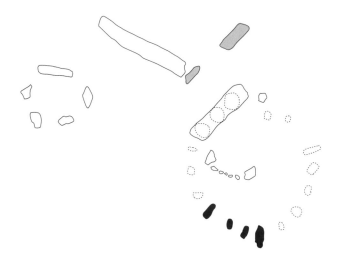

57
Kealkil
Co. Kerry

W 055 556
Six miles NNE of Bantry

On an untidy and unattractive area of moorland above Bantry Bay this is a neat megalithic collection of a stone circle, a pair of standing stones and a form of ring-cairn overlying the remnants of a second circle.

The first circle is tiny, an oval Five-Stone ring no more than 9 by 8 feet across, with a low recumbent block at the SW. When the site was excavated in 1938 two criss-crossing shallow trenches were uncovered, probably the surviving evidence of a heavy wooden base to support a tall central post.

Just to the NE are two pillars, close together and arranged NNE–SSW, one fallen, the other no less than 16 feet high but once much taller before it fell and broke in antiquity. A stump almost 4 feet long lies by it.

To the east of the Five-Stone ring is an irregularly round cairn with an open central space. Under it is a stuttering ring of low stones jutting from the perimeter like cogs. They may be the relics of a former stone circle over which a ring-cairn was carelessly and imperfectly superimposed. Only three scraps of scallop-shell were found there.

Other places of interest. Breeny More ruined circle, W 050 552, is 300 yards west.

58
Knocknakilla
Co. Cork

W 297 841
Eight miles NNW of Macroom

If ever there were carbon-copies in prehistory then Knocknakilla and Kealkil, 24 miles to the SW, separated by the River Sullane and the Sheey Mountains, were twins. Both complexes contained a Five-Stone ring, a pair of outlying stones and a ring-cairn.

Called *Knocknakilla*, "the stone church", because even in historic times it was believed to have been a place of worship, and also known as Muisire Beg, because the ring was raised on the lower slopes of Mushera Beg, this pleasing ring in state care is a Five-Stone circle, one of whose portals has fallen. With a recumbent stone "like a rough tombstone" but now prostrate, the ring was excavated in 1930, when masses of white quartz fragments were unearthed near the entrance. Not far to the SW was a once-imposing pair of stones, the nearer collapsed, the other still standing nearly 13 feet high. To the east is an overgrown ring-cairn, many of its kerbstones tumbled.

Other places of interest. Carriganimmy Five-Stone circle, W 293 827, is 3 miles south. Glantane recumbent stone circle, W 280 833, is 2 miles SSW.

This enchanting ring is now sadly closed to visitors

59
Lissyviggeen
Co. Kerry

V 997 906

Two miles east of Killarney

The *Lios* or "fairy-fort" is one of the petite sites in Ireland, a miniature combination of a variant of a recumbent stone circle inside a gross earthwork henge. Another charming name for this delight is The Seven Sisters.

Of the circle's seven small stones, bunched together like a lifeless ring-dance no more than 14 feet across, the lower, longer one at the south may be a half-remembered version of a recumbent slab. Around the ring is a rather scruffy earthen bank, 50 feet from side to side, with an entrance at the SSW. Outside it, 35 feet away, are two standing stones set east–west, vaguely in line with the equinoctial sunrise.

Other places of interest. This is an isolated site. Aghadoe twelfth-century church and 22-foot-high round tower, V 921 927, are 5 miles WNW. Kenmare variant recumbent stone circle, V 907 707, is 13¹/₂ miles SSW.

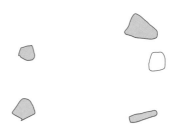

60

Lundin farm
Perthshire

NN 882 505
1³/₄ miles NE of Aberfeldy

This is a fine example of a Scottish "Four-Poster", a term invented as an archaeological joke but subsequently accepted as describing a widespread type of Bronze Age ring of four stones, often surrounding a central cremation. Such warped versions of stone circles are unlikely to be earlier than about 1600 BC, perhaps as late as 1200 BC in parts of south-western Ireland. The geometrical fact that the stones do not stand at the corners of a square or a rectangle but always conform to the circumference of a circle reveals their stone-circle ancestry.

Lundin Farm stands on a natural mound, but excavation in 1962 discovered a central pit against what may have been a pyre. In the hole were cremated human bones, the broken fragments of an urn with plaited-cord decoration around its neck, and some nondescript sherds of equally nondescript pots.

To the SE of the mound is a fallen slab with many artificial cupmarks ground out on it. The meaning of the art remains controversial, but an astronomical fact about the decorated Lundin Farm stone is that had it stood erect it would have been in line with the midwinter sunrise.

Other places of interest. Just north of the Four-Poster are the collapsed remains of another at NN 882 506. The small stone circle of *Tigh-na-Ruaich*, "the house in the heather", stands in a garden at NN 975 535, 6¹/₂ miles ENE.

61

Men an Tol
Cornwall

SW 426 349
3¹/₂ miles NW of Penzance

The *Men an Tol*, "the stone with a hole", is probably the most unlikely entry in this book about stone circles. Sometimes known as the Crick Stone or, worse, the Devil's Eye, this famous holed slab of granite stands on a quagmired moor near Land's End. It is generally believed that the 3-foot-8-inch-high rectangular slab with a 1-foot-6-inch hole bevelled through it had been the central feature of a simple 20-foot-long line, flanked by two 4-foot-tall stones. A third slab lies by it. Speculation that it had originally been the "portholed" entrance to a chambered tomb was mistaken. The nearest examples of such distinctive tombs are nearly two hundred miles away at Rodmarton and Avening in Gloucestershire.

There was a fifth stone 36 feet to the NW, with another lying nearby. The brilliant but tragic artist John Blight noticed them in 1864 and was the first to conjecture that the monument was the skeleton of a stone circle. He was ignored. The hole was too exciting in its own right.

As early as 1700 the slab was "famous for curing pains in the back by going through the hole, three, five or nine times". Naked children could supposedly be immunised against scrofula and rickets by being passed through it three times towards the sun and then dragged anti-clockwise – "widdershins" – three times around it. Boys were passed from a woman to a man, girls the reverse.

The stone had other qualities. Two brass pins laid crosswise on its upper edge had the power to answer any question. It was also claimed that through its hole the slab was aligned on the May and August sunrises to the ENE, and to the February and November sunsets to the

WSW. Others claimed that from the middle of the ring the Men an Tol, whether standing radially to the circumference or along it, was in line with the major rising of the southern moon.

Then, in 1992, there was an amazing discovery. The Cornwall Archaeological Unit located the evidence of a true circle, 56 to 59 feet across, of some twenty to twenty-two stones, numbers characteristic of Land's End rings. Other researchers recalculated the number of stones as nineteen. The Men an Tol stood at the SE, at right angles to the perimeter.

The perforation was probably natural. Lying on a nearby tor a saucerlike boulder had been exposed to a million rains whose waters gathered, seeped, eroded the centre away. Marvelling at the phenomenon, people in the Bronze Age took it, enhanced the hole and incorporated the magical block in their circle. Perhaps centuries later the northern edge of a burial-mound was laid reverently on it.

Other places of interest. Mulfra Quoit, SW 452 354, is 1¹/₂ miles east. Lanyon Quoit, SW 430 337, is ³/₄ miles south. Chysauster Late Iron Age village, SW 473 350, is 3 miles east.

62

Moel ty Uchaf
Gwynedd

SJ 057 371

1¹/₂ miles east of Llandrillo

Not quite at the top of the hill, at an altitude of 1375 feet O.D., is the almost perfect cairn-circle of Moel ty Uchaf, "the high, bare hill". About 39 feet across and slightly flattened at the north, it was perhaps meant to be seen from the valley below. It stands on a hillock. Some forty stones form its circumference, on average about 1 foot 6 inches tall. There is a probable entrance at the SSW. A finely preserved cist can be seen at its centre.

Eighty yards to the south and 50 feet lower down the slope are the cleared remains of a cairn from which much white quartz was recovered.

The ruinous circle of Tyfos can be seen in the valley bottom two miles to the NW at a height of 550 feet O.D. It is not on the horizon, but Alexander Thom suggested that with a compass-bearing of 298°.6 the declination is +16°.9, perhaps intended as a foresight on the May Day sunrise.

Other places of interest. There are cairns on Craig yr Arian, SJ 015 360, 3 miles SW.

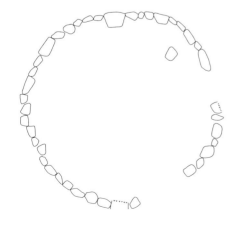

This little kerb-circle stands in a wide pasture field. Ten low granite boulders lie along the circumference of a circle only 16 feet 5 inches in diameter. Originally there may have been fifteen of these side-by-side stones. None is more than 2 feet high. Just to the SW is a large prostrate stone of metamorphosed grit, its upper surface profusely decorated with cup- and cup-and-ring marks. It was once connected to the circle by a rough 15-foot-long causeway of cobbles.

Excavation of the ring in 1938 found that the interior had been extensively burned by a fire of hazel wood. Just off-centre in a small cist was a little heap of the cremated bones of an adult and a young child. Two broken rims of flat-rimmed ware were found on the burnt surface of the ring. Fragments of white quartz had been scattered around the inner faces of the kerbstones.

Alexander Thom observed that from the cupmarked slab the midsummer sun would have been seen setting over a stone 5 feet high three hundred yards to the NW.

Other places of interest. Crofthead standing stones, NN 920 240, are 2¼ miles east. Fowlis Wester paired stone circles, NN 923 249, are 2½ miles ENE. Inchaffray Abbey, NN 956 225, is 4½ miles ESE. The remains and sites of Roman signal stations, a fort and road on the line of the Antonine Wall are about 3½ miles to the south and SE.

63

Monzie
Perthshire

NN 882 243

Two miles NE of Crieff

This unusual ring, possibly Scottish in origin even though in the far south of England, is also one of the most dangerous to visit. Ardblair in Perthshire is almost as bad, because it has a straight and fast road racing through the centre of it. The Nine Stones do not, but they are on the wrong side of the busy major highway of the A35 for anyone in a car, and care has to be taken, first walking from the lay-by, then crossing the road. At the end of the visit equal care has to be taken in reverse.

The ring is an ellipse about 30 feet north–south by 26 feet. Its surviving nine stones, one fallen, are a mixture of sarsen and conglomerate of which there are many in the locality. Seven of the stones are hardly 3 feet high, but at the NW are two giants, one with a pointed top 7 feet high, its partner 6 feet high and flat-topped, a characteristic conjunction of "male" and "female" stones whose symbolism remains unclear. It is arguable that once there was a low block between its "flankers" in an arrangement of an aberrant recumbent stone circle, for which there are counterparts in SW Scotland. Perhaps by coincidence, but probably not, there is a "Scottish" chambered tomb, the Grey Mare and Her Colts, only 2¹/₂ miles to the SW.

With decrepit railings imprisoning the ring, and with trees and bushes crowding around, the Nine Stones is one of the most difficult to photograph.

Other places of interest. The Grey Mare and Her Colts, of Clyde–Solway architecture, with a deeply concave forecourt, lies at SY 583 871, 2¹/₂ miles SW. The two elongated Long Bredy Neolithic bank barrows, SY 580 904, are 2 miles west. Maiden Castle hillfort, SY 668 885, is 3³/₄ miles ESE.

64
Nine stones
Winterbourne Abbas, Dorset

SY 611 904
Five miles west of Dorchester

65

Reanascreena
Co. Cork

W 265 410

7¹/₂ miles SSE of Dunmanway

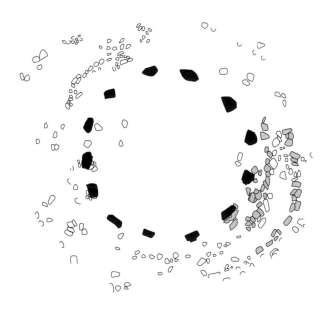

Overlooked by the dark hill of Carrigfadda and on the summit of another high hill, a distinctive feature of this recumbent stone circle, "the ring of the shrine", is its surrounding 12-foot-wide low earthen bank, with an equally broad but shallow ditch inside it like an uncertain version of a circle-henge. Altogether the site is 78 feet across, half-concealed in long, bristling grass.

The circle consists of twelve stones, two forming an ENE entrance with a recumbent opposite. The ring has a diameter of approximately 30 feet like Drombeg and Bohonagh. The axis is aligned ENE–WSW, neither to the equinoxes nor the solstices, but it may have been directed to the sunsets of early February and November, the prehistoric feast-days of Imbolc and Samain.

Near the centre of the circle was a pit filled with earth. Ten feet to the north was another, lined with a mixture of charcoal and scraps of cremated bone. Four pits with broken bones lay under the bank near the entrance. Prehistoric rebuilding near there was thought to show that the site had continued in use after its dedication.

Like Drombeg, it was a very late circle. Two radiocarbon determinations of 830±35 bc and 945±35 bc suggest a period for Reanascreena around 1050 BC, but as the "dates" came from an intrusive central burial the ring may have been set up several centuries earlier.

Other places of interest. There is a remarkable concentration and variety of stone circles within 3 miles of the site: a recumbent stone circle at Carrigagrenane, W 254 432; a Five-Stone ring at Lettergorman South-West, W 262 456; and a Four-Poster, Lettergorman North-East, W 267 473.

66
Reenkilla
Co. Kerry

V 768 577

1¹/₂ miles SSW of Lauragh

Only the adventurous see this strange Four-Poster, for it is hidden in woodland on the miniature landlocked island of Knockcappul on the south side of the River Kenmare. To reach it one must cross the tidal estuary, not far but dangerous except for the brief period of low tide. The place is also known as Hangman's Island from the eighteenth-century gallows that once stood concealed in the trees.

The visit is worth it. *Reenkilla*, "the church on the headland", a distorted ring but in good condition, has its four stones at the corners of a very irregular quadrilateral, the disproportionate NE pillar being 8 feet high and twice the height of the next tallest. Just to the north is a predictable outlying pillar.

Other places of interest. There are nearby recumbent stone circles: Shronebirran, V 753 554, 2 miles SSW; Drombohilly, V 790 607, 2¹/₂ miles NNE; and Ardgroom, V 707 553, 4¹/₂ miles SW.

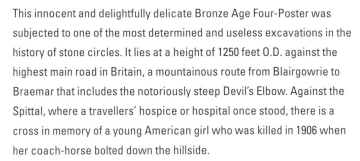

This innocent and delightfully delicate Bronze Age Four-Poster was subjected to one of the most determined and useless excavations in the history of stone circles. It lies at a height of 1250 feet O.D. against the highest main road in Britain, a mountainous route from Blairgowrie to Braemar that includes the notoriously steep Devil's Elbow. Against the Spittal, where a travellers' hospice or hospital once stood, there is a cross in memory of a young American girl who was killed in 1906 when her coach-horse bolted down the hillside.

The four low boulders form the corners of a rectangle 12 feet square, but they actually lie on the circumference of a true circle 17 feet in diameter. They sit like resting birds on a large oval mound 60 by 46 feet and at least 15 feet high. Locally it was known as Diarmid's Grave, the tomb of the legendary Celtic warrior who was slain by his foster-brother, an enchanted boar of Ben Bulbenn in Co. Sligo. As Sligo is some three hundred miles SW of Glenshee this was magic of impressive power.

Because the tomb was suspected of containing treasure, the centre of the Four-Poster was dug into on 28 August 1894. Below the topsoil there was yellow earth until, ten feet down, it became mixed with black patches of rotted peat. By the third day the diggers were becoming doubtful of finding anything and their misgivings increased at a depth of 17 feet, when the darkening earth began emitting a foul stench. A day later, 22 feet down, they gave up. They were sensible. The "tomb" was no more than a natural glacial moraine of which there were others in the neighbourhood. Bronze Age people had taken advantage of it to construct their ritual monument, as customary, on an upstanding mound. Unusually, they had buried nothing there. And if they had, their pit and its deposits would have been no more than 3 to 4 feet deep.

Other places of interest. There is a second Diarmid's Grave a hundred yards away. It is said to cover a gold cup. It does not. There are nearby Four-Posters: Broughdarg, NO 138 671, 2¹/₂ miles SE; and a cluster 12 miles to the south at Craighall Mill, NO 185 401; Parkneuk, NO 195 515; and Woodside, NO 185 501.

67
Spittal of Glenshee
Perthshire

NO 117 702

13¹/₂ miles NE of Pitlochry

Over a little bridge and across fields, between the two loughs of Cloonee and Inchquin, the unusual Five-Stone ring of *Uragh*, "the land of yews", stands in a wonderful setting on a low hill. It is lovely. Vainly dug into by uninformed treasure-hunters, the circle has a low recumbent, resembling an inverted guillotine blade, that is visually overwhelmed by a gigantic, broad outlying block only 2 feet behind the circle and a full 10 feet high. If the little ring was later than the thick pillar, then the circle-builders had no interest in any astronomical event behind their dwarfed recumbent.

Other places of interest. The recumbent stone circles of Drombohilly, V 790 607, and Dromroe, V 880 657, are 3¹/₂ miles SW and NE respectively.

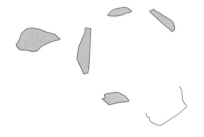

68

Uragh
Co. Kerry

V 832 635
4¹/₂ miles NNE of Lauragh

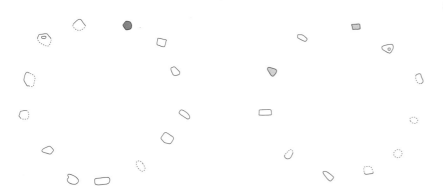

Beyond the five rings of Burn Moor looms Scafell Pike, England's highest peak

69
White Moss
Cumberland

NY 172 023, NY 173 024
6¹/₂ miles NE of Ravenglass

On the heights of Burn Moor above Eskdale the pair of rings known as White Moss are a quarter of a mile south of another pair at Low Longrigg but only 120 yards west of the fine Brats Hill stone circle, with its similarity to Castlerigg.

The two rings, both of local granite but in poor condition, are about one hundred feet apart on a WSW–ENE axis that has no apparent astronomical significance. The western site is some 55 feet in diameter, with a small, untidy cairn at its centre. Its partner is rather smaller, about 52 feet across, and also encloses a cairn.

On the plateau there are many cairns, which may be the result of land-clearance rather than of numerous burials, and to the east are the remains of an unenclosed platform settlement with field-systems and a droveway.

Other places of interest. The two Low Longrigg rings are 150 feet NE at NY 172 028 and NY 172 027. The fine Brats Hill stone circle, with its internal cairns, is at NY 173 023, 340 feet to the SE.

70
Yellowmead
Dartmoor,
Devon

SX 575 678
Seven miles SE of Tavistock

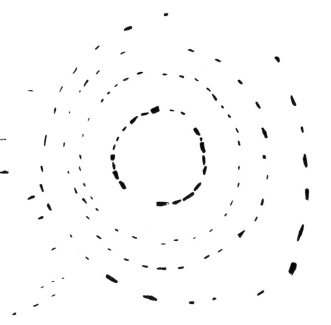

At the end of a book in which the great diversity of stone circles has been portrayed, it is entirely fitting that this site, the third generation of a series of mixed marriages, shows the greatest diversity of all. This is not a stone circle. It is four, one within the other, "a classic example of a Dartmoor multiple-ring variant". It lies a mile east of Sheepstor hamlet on Yellowmead Down. The area is one of many antiquities, "for the Saxons were a superstitious race, and were afraid of the settlements of the people they conquered".

Sheepstor has nothing to do with sheep. The name derives from the Celtic *syth*, "steep", and the tor is indeed a 1210-feet height of stone-slithering steepness, one of the most prominent on Dartmoor. From the east its outline looks like a resting lion, and from its crest there is a marvelling panorama of moorland, wooded valleys with sycamores and hazels, trickling streams and the eroded pyramids of other tors, Leather, Down and Coombeshead.

Half a mile south of the height is one of the strangest of all stone circles. Circles within circles are comparatively uncommon on Dartmoor, although there is a well-known one at Shovel Down to the west of Chagford, and at least eight others are recorded, including one at Drizzlecombe only a mile SW of Yellowmead.

Because of nature's unintended protection Yellowmead is better. Buried under peat it was not noticed until 1921, so late that no legends attach to it. In the drought of that year amongst the high heather and whortleberry scrub the fine Dartmoor antiquarian and polymath R. Hansford Worth recognised humps of buried stones lying in a circle that included one tall and two lower slabs jutting from the moor.

That autumn the Dartmoor Preservation Society excavated and reconstructed the site. The work was "very faithfully done", although three stones in the inner and two in the outer ring appear to be upside down. To the workers' amazement the unearthed stone circle had three more inside it. The outermost, composed of heavy boulders, was irregular, roughly 66 by 63 feet, with gaps where stones had been taken for a nearby wall and a bridge over a stream. At the SE the largest of the blocks was thought to have two or three cupmarks on its top, but these were natural depressions. Inside the ring was a second, also irregular and of smaller stones. As the two inner rings were circular and shared a common centre it was concluded that they were the denuded outlines of a kerbed cairn inside a surrounding stone circle.

The innermost ring, 22 feet across, had thick and heavy slabs shoulder to shoulder around a vestigial central mound. The Rev. Hugh Breton, one of the enthusiastic volunteers, speculated that "it encircled the burial-place of some king or powerful chief of pre-historic times". It is likely that this was the original monument, an encircled cairn to which later rings were added eccentrically, with the beginnings of multiple rows extending to the WSW. They have been grossly robbed for a tin-miners' leat and a wall. Yellowmead is an intriguing rarity but it is not the only curiosity at Sheepstor. Half a mile west, amongst a jostle of huge, tumbled boulders at the south end of the tor, is the Pixies' House, a long narrow cave concealed under a granite overhang. Pins were left there to appease the spiteful elves.

More afraid of prowling Roundheads than of the little people, the cavalier Squire Elford, whose family gave Yelverton its name, hid there during the Civil War. His tenants fed him in his dark and damp refuge. On bright days as sunlight filtered dimly into the gloom he must have wondered at the miraculous green iridescence glittering from the tiny fronds of luminous moss, *schistostega osmundacea*, that grew on the walls of his cavern.

It is fitting to end with such thoughts, for this has been a book of attractive stone circles that have been photographed with a rare luminosity. The volume is a thing of loveliness itself.

Other places of interest. Drizzlecombe rows and circles, SX 592 671, are 1¼ miles ESE. Down Tor circle and rows, SX 587 694, are 1¼ NE. Legis Tor pound settlement, SX 570 654, is 1½ miles south.

Acknowledgements

I would like to thank the following companies and individuals for their generous sponsorship and personal interest: Helen James at **Kodak Professional Imaging**, all the front desk staff at **Kodachrome** Wimbledon, Uli Hinter of **Leica Cameras**, Matt Graydon of **Irish Sea Operations** and **Seacat Ferries**, Amanda Woollacott of **Vistacon/Acuvue** contact lenses, **Vango** camping equipment, **Innovations** and **Hawkshead** clothing, **Orkney Tourist Board, Aberdeenshire Tourist Board**, **The Irish Tourist Board**, **Boyd & Co** and all the team at **Genesis** photo lab of Fulham, especially Ken Sethi and Phil Holding.

Those who contributed to the progress of this project number in the high hundreds and include all the landowners who granted me access to their property, those people met at remote sites who asked if they were in the way, and many who supplied snippets of information and folklore or simply wished me good luck. I am grateful to them all.
I am especially indebted to the following people, who repeatedly provided bed and banquet at ungodly hours as I returned to catch the changing seasons:
The Norths of Batworthy, Waghorns of Hampton Court, Bernards of Ashiestel, Flynns of Vellynsaudry, Corbetts of Chipping Camden, Robertsons of Culag and Stirling, O'Learys of Carriganimma, Willsons of Drombohilly, Mills of Under Loughrigg, Prenderghasts of Stromness and Langhams of Tempo. Also Rose Fitzjohn in Kildare and David Munro of the Findhorn Foundation.

Pru Piper kindly lent me books on the subject and showed me the black and white Circle Stone photographs by her late husband Edward, Charles and Anne Findlay hosted a week on Lewis where the Callanish shots began the book in earnest, Stephen Fulford provided a luxurious headquarters in South Kensington and Neil and Vicky Fox provided helicopter flights and teacakes. To each of them I express my profound gratitude.

At the earliest stages of my photographic career several people gave me valuable advice and critical encouragement. Among these I would like to thank Danny Pope, Zelda Cheatle, Mark Holborn, Ian Dickensand Wolfgang Schüler.

I would especially like to thank my family, Mhairi, Mark and Louise, Nicko and Victoria, Melissa and Brett, Richard and my aunt Sheila Mundle as well as Susi Boyd, Chris Humphries, Sam North, Simon Newson, Jamie Robertson, Victoria Upton, Stephen Fulford and Mary Findlay for their love, support and innumerable kindness over the years.

The team assembled by Christopher MacLehose at Harvill made the entire process a joy. Their dedication, goodwill and obvious love of books are any author's dream. Sophie Henley-Price has been a wonderful editor and, with the designer Isambard Thomas, made judgements that greatly enhanced my original ideas. Christopher himself has been a benign presence as ever.

Finally I must thank the two people who helped get the book started when it was merely a dream: Aubrey Burl whose expertise and frame of reference were matched by his generosity of spirit and humour, and Jane Turnbull, my literary agent, whose enthusiasm and frankness I treasure.

Note

Throughout this project I used LEICA camera equipment and KODAK film. Specifically R6 camera bodies, with 24mm, 35mm, 60mm/macro, 90mm and 250mm lenses. The vast majority of pictures, including twenty minute moonlit exposures, were shot on Kodachrome 64, with Ektachrome E200 pushed one stop for trickier twilight. All the photographs were taken in natural or available light, without the use of filters, flash or any subsequent manipulation.

For further information about forthcoming exhibitions, lectures and photographic projects please visit the website at:
www.maxmilligan.com

Bibliography

For readers wanting further details of sites in this book, including references to surveys and excavations, the most convenient source is the writer's *Guide to the Stone Circles of Britain, Ireland and Brittany*, Yale University Press, 1995. The Gazetteer in the writer's *The Stone Circles of the British Isles*, Yale University Press, 1976, has an extended list of sources. A second, updated and expanded edition is due for publication in AD 2000.

Other very useful and interesting books for readers wanting to explore further aspects of stone circles are given below.

Barber, C., *Mysterious Wales*, Paladin, London, 1983

– *More Mysterious Wales*, David & Charles, Newton Abbot, 1986

Barnatt, J., *Prehistoric Cornwall. The Ceremonial Monuments*, Turnstone, Wellingborough, 1982

– *Stone Circles of Britain, I, II*, British Archaeological Reports, Oxford, 1989

– *The Henges, Stone Circles and Ringcairns of the Peak District*, University of Sheffield, Sheffield, 1990

Bord, J. & C., *Mysterious Britain*, Paladin, St Albans, 1974

– *Atlas of Magical Britain*, Sidgwick & Jackson, London, 1990

Bowen, E. G. & Gresham, C. A., *History of Merioneth, I. From the Earliest Times to the Age of the Native Princes*, Merioneth Historical & Record Society, Dolgellau, 1967

Bradley, R., *Rock Art and the Prehistory of Atlantic Europe*, Routledge, London, 1997

– "The Significance of Monuments. On the Shaping of Human Experience" in *Neolithic and Bronze Age Europe*, Routledge, London, 1998

Brown, P. L., *Megaliths, Myths and Men*, Blandford Press, Poole, 1976

Burgess, C., *The Age of Stonehenge*, J. M. Dent, London, 1980

Burl, A., *The Stone Circles of the British Isles*, Yale University Press, London, 1976

— *Prehistoric Avebury*, Yale University Press, London, 1979

— *Prehistoric Stone Circles*, Shire Publications, Princes Risborough, 1979

— *Prehistoric Astronomy and Ritual*, Shire Publications, Princes Risborough, 1983

— *The Stonehenge People*, J. M. Dent, London, 1987

— *Four-Posters. Bronze Age Stone Circles of Western Europe*, British Archaeological Reports, Oxford, 1988

— *Guide to the Stone Circles of Britain, Ireland and Brittany*, Yale University Press, London, 1995

— *Great Stone Circles*, Yale University Press, London, 1999

Butler, J., *Dartmoor Atlas of Antiquities*, volumes 1–5, Devon Books, Tiverton, 1991–1997

Castleden, R., *Neolithic Britain. New Stone Age Sites of England, Scotland and Wales*, Routledge, London, 1992

— *The Making of Stonehenge*, Routledge, London, 1993

Chippindale, C., *Stonehenge Complete*, 2nd edition, Thames & Hudson, London, 1994

Cleal, R. M. J., Walker, K. E. & Montague, R. (eds), *Stonehenge in its Landscape*, English Heritage, London, 1995

Cles-Reden, S. von, *The Realm of the Great Goddess*, Thames & Hudson, London, 1961

Cooney, G. & Grogan, E. *Irish Prehistory: a Social Perspective*, Wordwell, Dublin, 1994

Darvill, T., *Prehistoric Britain*, Batsford, London, 1987

Devereux, P. & Thomson, I., *The Ley Hunter's Companion*, Thames & Hudson, London, 1979

Dyer. J., *The Penguin Guide to Prehistoric England and Wales*, Allen Lane, London, 1981

— *Ancient Britain*, Batsford, London, 1980

Evans, E., *Prehistoric and Early Christian Ireland. A Guide*, Batsford, London, 1966

Feachem, R., *Guide to Prehistoric Scotland*, Batsford, London, 1977

Gelling, M., *Place-Names in the Landscape. The Geographical Roots of Britain's Place-Names*, J. M. Dent, London, 1984

Gibson, A., *Stonehenge and Timber Circles*, Tempus, Oxford, 1998

Gibson, A. & Simpson, D. D. A. (eds), *Prehistoric Ritual and Religion*, Alan Sutton, Thrupp, 1998

Graham, J. T., *British Megaliths. A Bibliographical Guide*, Hatfield Polytechnic, Hatfield, 1981

Grinsell, L. V., *Folklore of Prehistoric Sites in Britain*, David & Charles, London, 1976

Guiley, R. E., *The Lunar Almanac*, Piatkus, London, 1991

Hadingham, E., *Ancient Carvings in Britain. A Mystery*, Garnstone Press, London, 1974

— *Circles and Standing Stones*, Heinemann, London, 1975

Harbison, P., *Pre-Christian Ireland. From the First Settlers to the Celts*, Thames & Hudson, London, 1988

— *Guide to National and Historic Monuments of Ireland*, Gill & Macmillan, Dublin, 1992

Hawkes, J. & Bahn, P., *The Shell Guide to Archaeology*, Michael Joseph, London, 1986

Heggie, D. C., *Megalithic Science. Ancient Mathematics and Astronomy in Northwest Europe*, Thames & Hudson, London, 1981

Hollier, J., *Nothing but Circles. Map and Guide to the Stone Circles of England, Scotland and Wales*, J. Hollier, Crewkerne, 1989

Houlder, C., *Wales: an Archaeological Guide. The Prehistoric, Roman and Early Medieval Field Monuments*, Faber & Faber, London, 1974

Lambrick, G., *The Rollright Stones. Megaliths, Monuments, and Settlement in the Prehistoric Landscape*, English Heritage, Oxford, 1988

Lockyer, Sir N., *Stonehenge and other British Stone Monuments Astronomically Considered*, 2nd ed., Macmillan, London, 1909

MacKie, E. W., *Science and Society in Prehistoric Britain*, Elek, London, 1977

McCrickard, J., *Eclipse of the Sun. An Investigation into Sun and Moon Myths*, Gothic Image, Glastonbury, 1990

McMann, J., *Riddles of the Stone Age. Rock Carvings of Ancient Europe*, Thames & Hudson, London, 1980

Megaw, J. V. S. & Simpson, D. D. A., *Introduction to British Prehistory*, University of Leicester, Leicester, 1979

Michell, J., *The Old Stones of Land's End*, Garnstone Press, London, 1974

— *Megalithomania*, Thames & Hudson, London, 1982

— *A Little History of Astro-Archaeology. Stages in the Transformation of a Heresy*, 2nd ed., Thames & Hudson, London, 1989

O'Kelly, M., *Early Ireland. An Introduction to Irish Prehistory*, Cambridge University Press, Cambridge, 1989

O'Nuallain, S., *Stone Circles in Ireland*, Country House, Dublin, 1995

Opie. I. & Tatem, M. (eds), *A Dictionary of Superstitions*, Oxford University Press, Oxford, 1989

O'Riordain, S. P., *Antiquities of the Irish Countryside*, Methuen, London, 1964

O'Sullivan, M., *Megalithic Art in Ireland*, Country House, Dublin, 1993

Pepper, E. & Wilcock. J., *Magical and Mystical Sites. Europe and the British Isles*, Abacus, London, 1978

Reader's Digest, *Folklore, Myths and Legends of Britain*, Reader's Digest, London, 1973

Room, A., *Dictionary of Place-Names in the British Isles*, Bloomsbury Press, London, 1988

Ryan. M. (ed.), *The Illustrated Archaeology of Ireland*, Country House, Dublin, 1991

Service, A. & Bradbery, J., *The Standing Stones of Europe. A Guide to the Great Megalithic Monuments*, J. M. Dent, London, 1993

Spooner, G. M. & Russell, F. S. (eds), *Worth's Dartmoor*, David & Charles, Newton Abbot, 1967

Thom, A., *Megalithic Sites in Britain*, Oxford University Press, Oxford, 1967

Thom, A. S. & Burl, A., *Megalithic Rings. Plans and Data for 229 Sites in Britain*, British Archaeological Reports, Oxford, 1980

Waterhouse, J., *The Stone Circles of Cumbria*, Phillimore, Chichester, 1985

Westwood, J., *Albion. A Guide to Legendary Britain*, Grafton, London, 1987

Whitlock, R., *In Search of Lost Gods. A Guide to British Folklore*, Phaidon Press, Oxford, 1979

Williamson, T. & Bellamy, L., *Ley Lines in Question*, World's Work, Kingswood, 1982

Wood, J. E., *Sun, Moon and Standing Stones*, Oxford University Press, Oxford, 1978

Index

Note: **Emboldened** page numbers indicate major entries and illustrations